ARKIVIA BOOKS

Published by
**ARKIVIA BOOKS** srl

Via Provinciale , 68
24022 Alzano Lombardo
Bergamo  ( Italy )
Phone:
(0039) 035515851
web:
www.arkiviabooks.com
www.vincenzosguera.com
e-mail:
info@arkiviabooks.com
info@vincenzosguera.com

The DVD included is free,
it is an integral part of this
publication and cannot be
sold separately.

The use of designs included
in this book and in the DVD is free.
The copyright of the designs belongs
to Vincenzo Sguera, who does not
transfer an exclusive use.
Include a line, indicating the copyright
credit, everywhere possible.
The republication of this book in part
or in whole and with any kind of
medium (paper, CD, DVD, photocopier
Internet etc.) is forbidden except by
a reviewer who may quote brief passages
in a review.
The creation of designs is
a continuously evolving activity.
Any resemblance between
the designs in this book
and other designs subject
to intellectual-property copyright
results from ignorance
of the existence of said copyright
or is purely coincidental.
If, unknown to the authors and the
publisher, any design contained
in this book is already registered,
they do not authorize the use
of such design by book buyers.
They decline all responsability since
they cannot be aware of all the designs
registered or used previous to this
publication in all countries.

Copyright © 2013
Vincenzo Sguera

## Some Explanations on Copyright

ARKIVIA BOOKS is not responsible
for the use of its designs where
this does not conform to the laws in
force to which the user is subject.
Users assume  full responsibility and
should verify the real possibilities of use
in their own territory of production,
distribution and sales.

All the designs in this book are ready
for production and the use is free.
This is really important:
Those who buy this book can use freely
the designs inside with only 3 reserves:

1)
they may not use the designs to produce
a book with the same purpose and may
not sell the designs in internet website.

note: they may sell their products derived
from these designs but not the designs
themselves

2)
they must respect the destination of
the designs.
So if a design is a texture, a different use
is not authorized, such as a trademark;
the same is valid for characters or
graphics suitable for printing on T-shirts
These designs are merely ornamental designs.

3)
Mention the copyright © Vincenzo Sguera
with the year of edition of this book.

Copyright belongs to Vincenzo Sguera
who in this case cedes the use,
apart from the reserves mentioned.
Thus, these designs are
not "copyright free" but  "use free".

# DVD info / Technical Details

The Book contains 1 DVD with 5 FOLDERS, suitable for WINDOWS® and MACINTOSH®.

TYPE OF FILES

The Files contained in the FOLDERS AI/EPS are all VECTOR :
this means in the first place that they can be opened by all softwares that use VECTOR Design. It is made up of exact lines that delimit areas where the color is uniform.
This enables the design to be brought to any size while retaining the maximum quality required.
The Files contained in the FOLDER PDF and the FOLDER JPG are all BITMAP .

SOFTWARE

The main VECTOR softwares are :
ILLUSTRATOR (the first came out in 1988), CORELDRAW and FREEHAND.
The BITMAP files (FOLDERS PDF, JPG) can be opened in software such as PHOTOSHOP, CORELPAINT, PAINTSHOP, COREL PAINTER etc..

SIZES

The size of the files is reported near the designs.

COLORS

In VECTOR files the single colors are flat, without transparencies or shading off.
By changing the Four Color percentages they can be modified within the software.
Each single color can be saved to prepare films, calenders, looms.

The colors used are 2: BLACK and WHITE

Warning:
to avoid possible production problems with the vector files, I suggest you deactivate the overprint option, because the colors are flat and are not overprinted.

The copyright of WINDOWS, MACINTOSH, ILLUSTRATOR, CORELDRAW, FREEHAND, PHOTOSHOP, CORELPAINT, PAINTSHOP, COREL PAINTER belongs to the owners.

CONTENT:

There are 5 FOLDERS and each one has a different format and contains the same 160 designs but with different characteristics. In total there are 800 Files

FOLDER AI v.CS4
These Files are in AI Format saved for Illustrator CS4.

FOLDER AI v.10
There are all the designs with the same characteristics as FOLDER AI v.CS4 but saved for ILLUSTRATOR 10.

FOLDER EPS v.8
These Files are in EPS Format saved for Illustrator 8. Being a old format, it is useful for people who have old versions of ILLUSTRATOR or FREEHAND or CORELDRAW.

FOLDER TIFF 500dpi (bitmap)
For those who want to have TIFF Files without tones of gray, they are in this FOLDER.

FOLDER JPG 150dpi
Here you can find Low Resolution BITMAP Files in JPG format (150 DPI in RGB color scale), that can be used to develop projects with lighter Files to speed up work and are for quick vision.

All files can be opened by:
ILLUSTRATOR 8 and following
CORELDRAW 10 and following
FREEHAND 9 and following
PHOTOSHOP in any version.

# THE BEAUTY OF A SCRIBBLE

The absolute beauty of a blot or a doodle is due to freedom of movement, free to express its uncertainty.

Completely random, with no intelligible rules it expresses an absolute, specular to the perfection of the geometry of a circle or a square.
The mind can easily see countless meanings and project its own needs or mental processes.
By doing so it resolves the sense of stress of not knowing what the abstract and meaningless thing is.
It cannot exist without and our psyche says that it has a meaning, that's easier, more comfortable for us:
visual and psychological problem solving.
The affirmation of self, who we are, also passes through the interpretations of abstract images.

Now art is full of these signs and we have learned that they can be intelligible and part of our culture, in a word, beautiful.

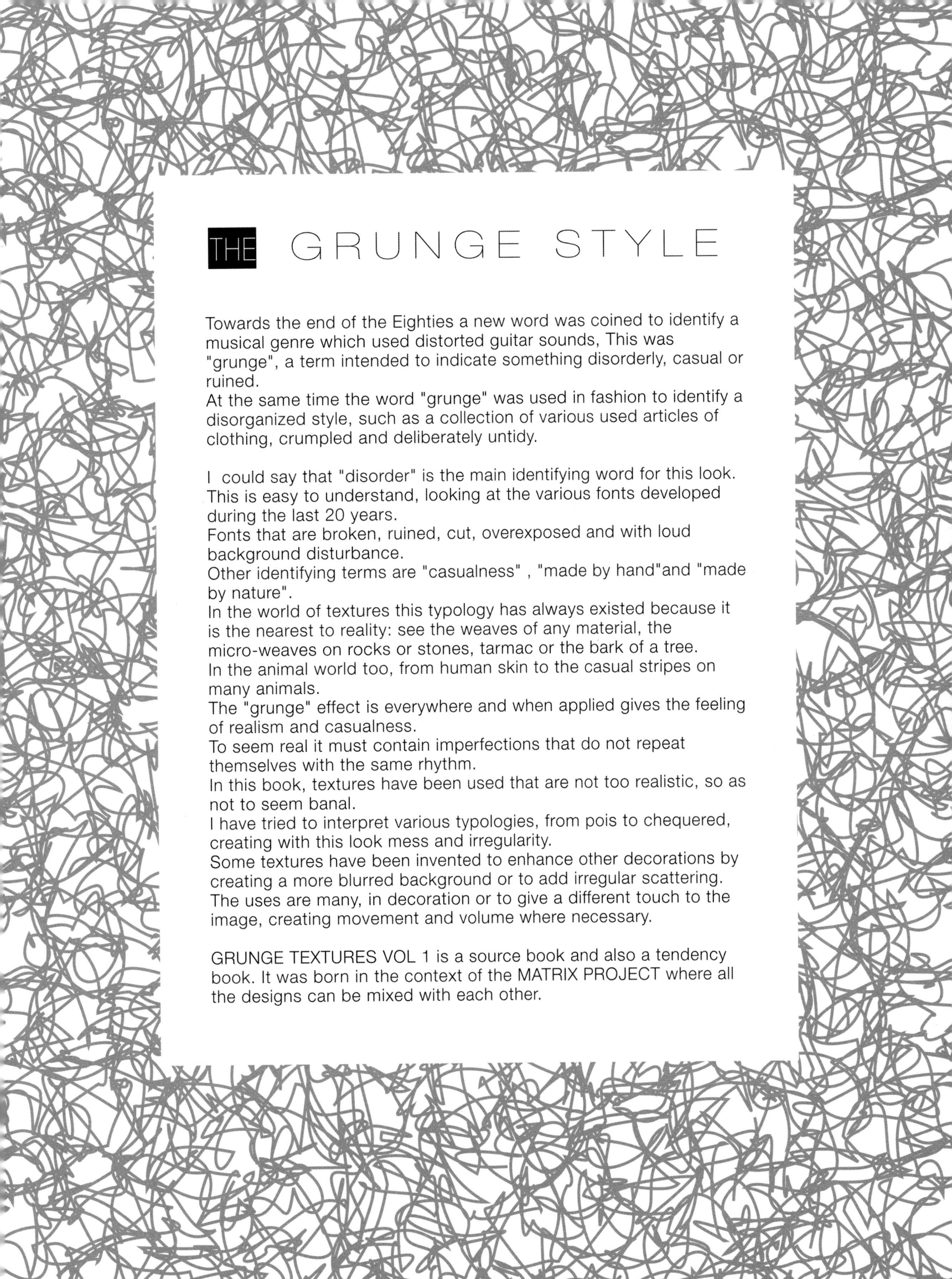

# THE GRUNGE STYLE

Towards the end of the Eighties a new word was coined to identify a musical genre which used distorted guitar sounds, This was "grunge", a term intended to indicate something disorderly, casual or ruined.
At the same time the word "grunge" was used in fashion to identify a disorganized style, such as a collection of various used articles of clothing, crumpled and deliberately untidy.

I could say that "disorder" is the main identifying word for this look. This is easy to understand, looking at the various fonts developed during the last 20 years.
Fonts that are broken, ruined, cut, overexposed and with loud background disturbance.
Other identifying terms are "casualness", "made by hand" and "made by nature".
In the world of textures this typology has always existed because it is the nearest to reality: see the weaves of any material, the micro-weaves on rocks or stones, tarmac or the bark of a tree.
In the animal world too, from human skin to the casual stripes on many animals.
The "grunge" effect is everywhere and when applied gives the feeling of realism and casualness.
To seem real it must contain imperfections that do not repeat themselves with the same rhythm.
In this book, textures have been used that are not too realistic, so as not to seem banal.
I have tried to interpret various typologies, from pois to chequered, creating with this look mess and irregularity.
Some textures have been invented to enhance other decorations by creating a more blurred background or to add irregular scattering.
The uses are many, in decoration or to give a different touch to the image, creating movement and volume where necessary.

GRUNGE TEXTURES VOL 1 is a source book and also a tendency book. It was born in the context of the MATRIX PROJECT where all the designs can be mixed with each other.

GT0001
pattern size
20 cm x 20 cm

GT0002
pattern size
16 cm x 20 cm

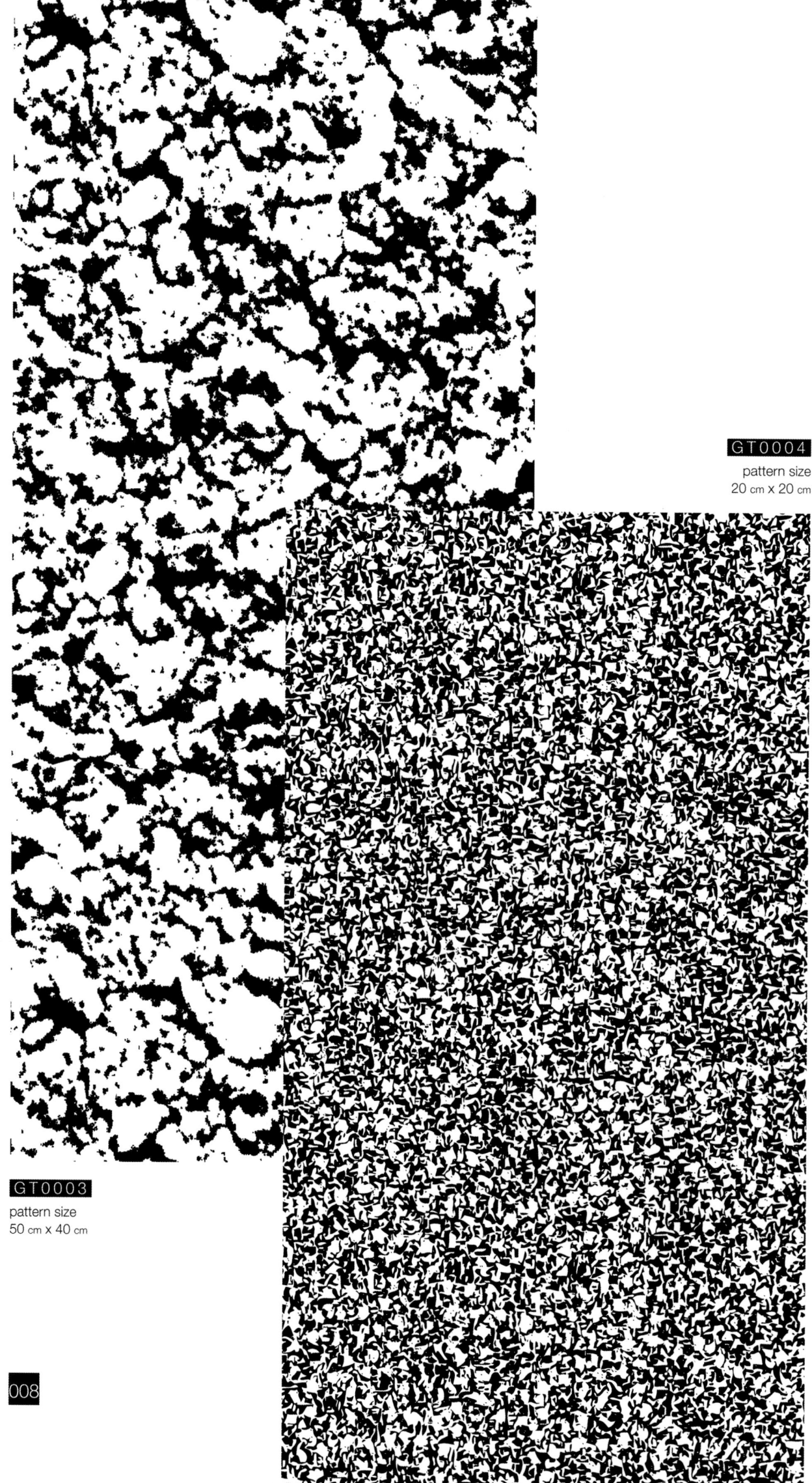

GT0004
pattern size
20 cm x 20 cm

GT0003
pattern size
50 cm x 40 cm

GT0005
pattern size
30 cm x 30 cm

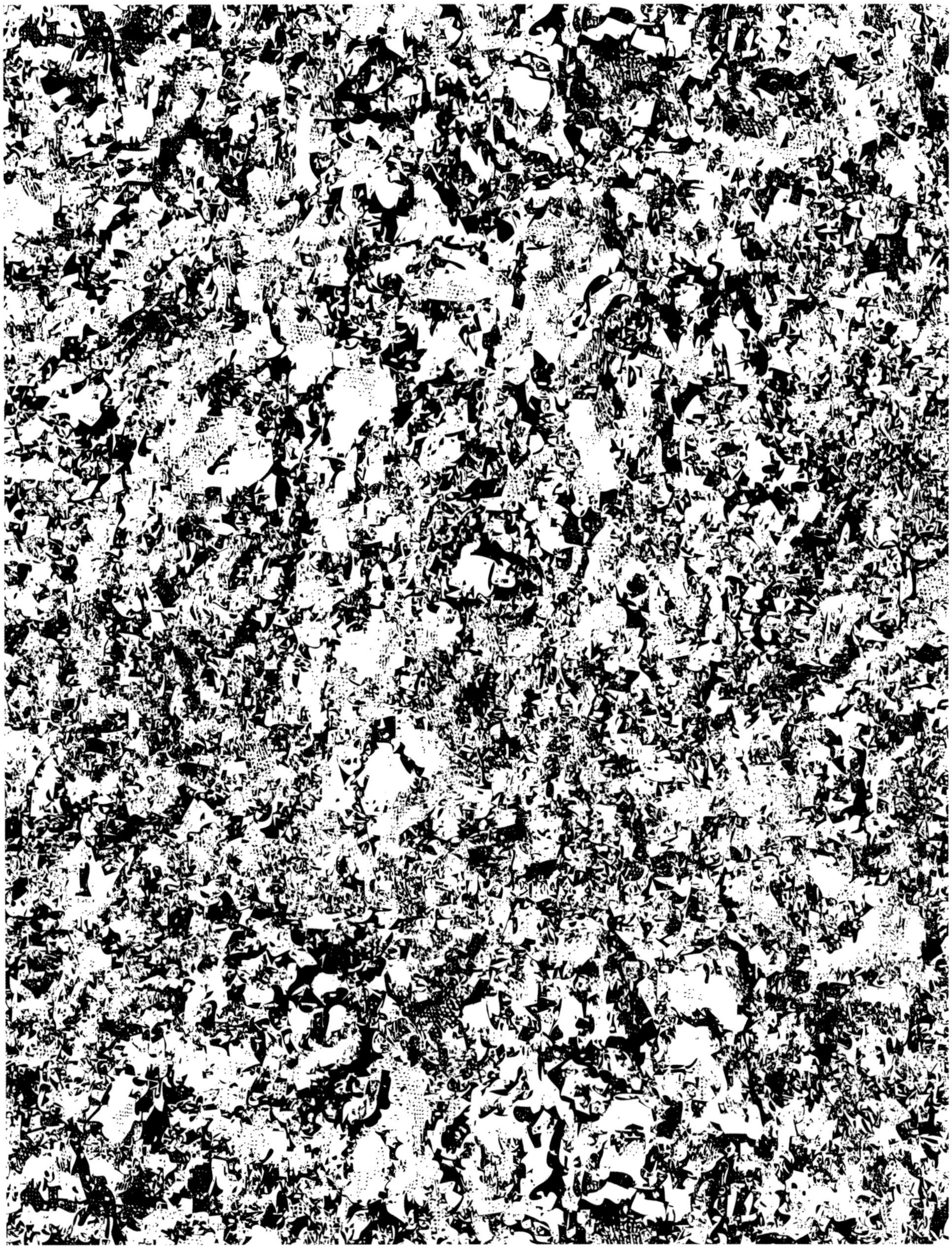

GT0006
pattern size
20 cm x 20 cm

GT0007

pattern size
30 cm x 30 cm

## GT0008
pattern size
25 cm x 25 cm

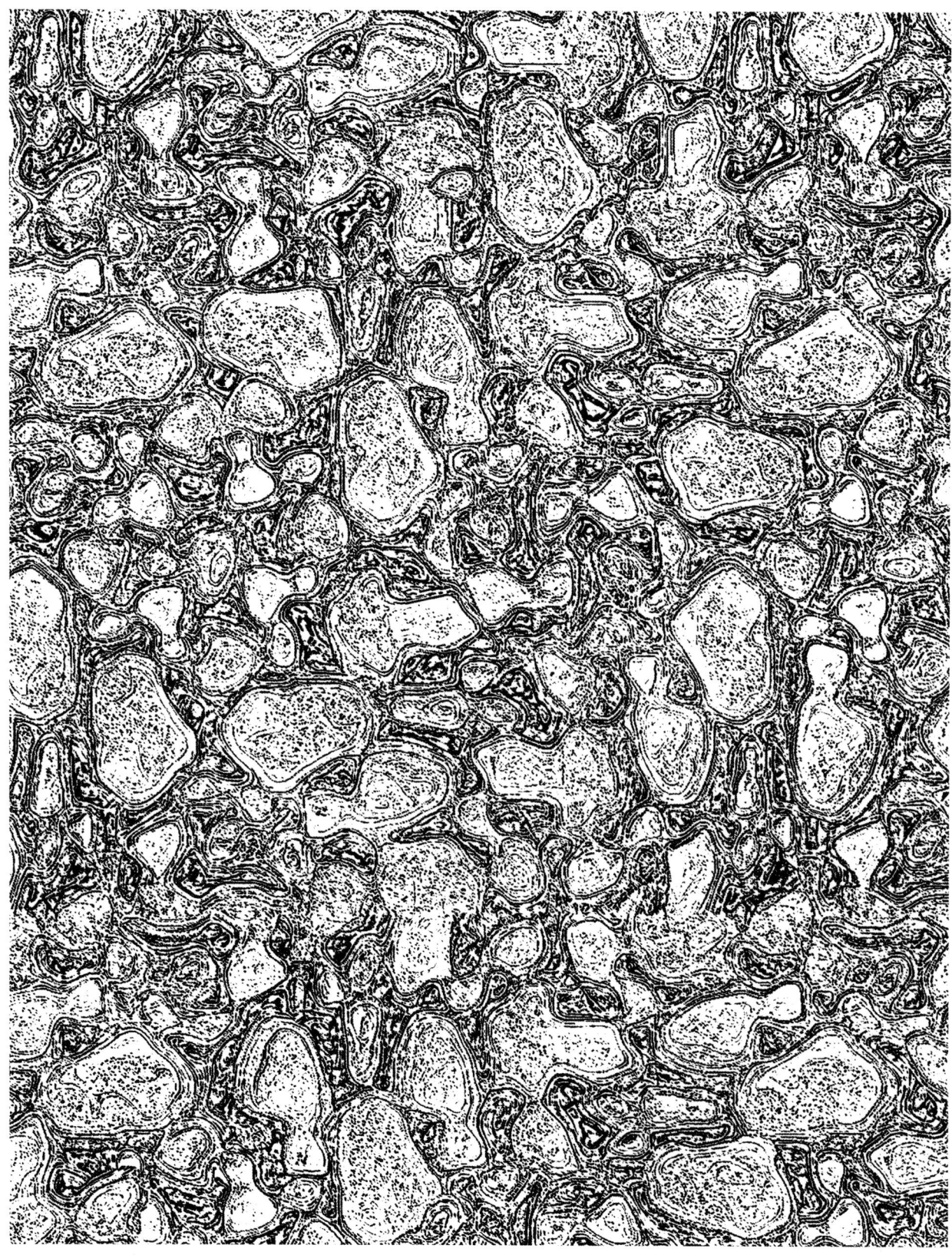

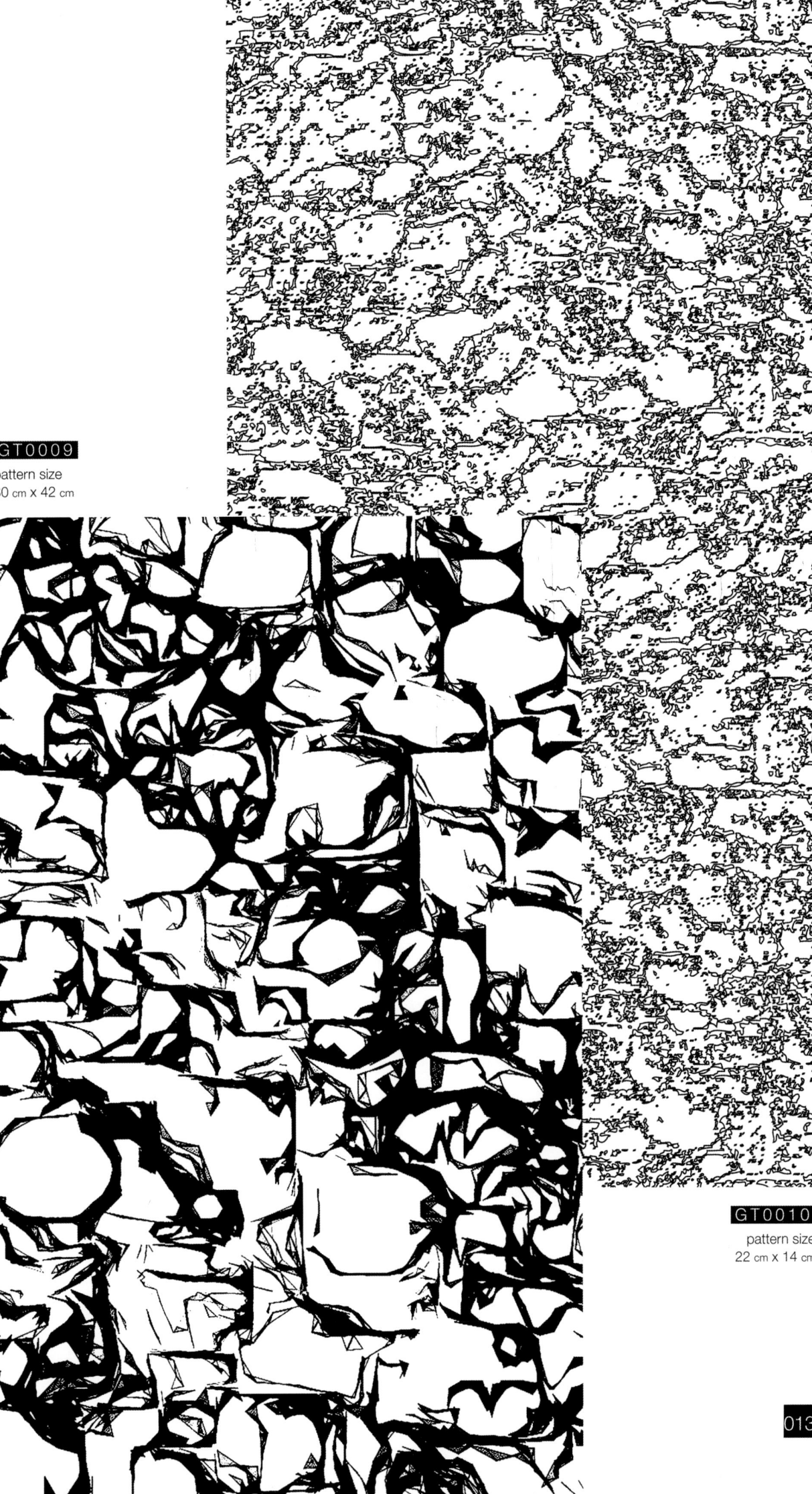

GT0009
pattern size
30 cm x 42 cm

GT0010
pattern size
22 cm x 14 cm

## GT0011

pattern size
28,2 cm x 28,2 cm

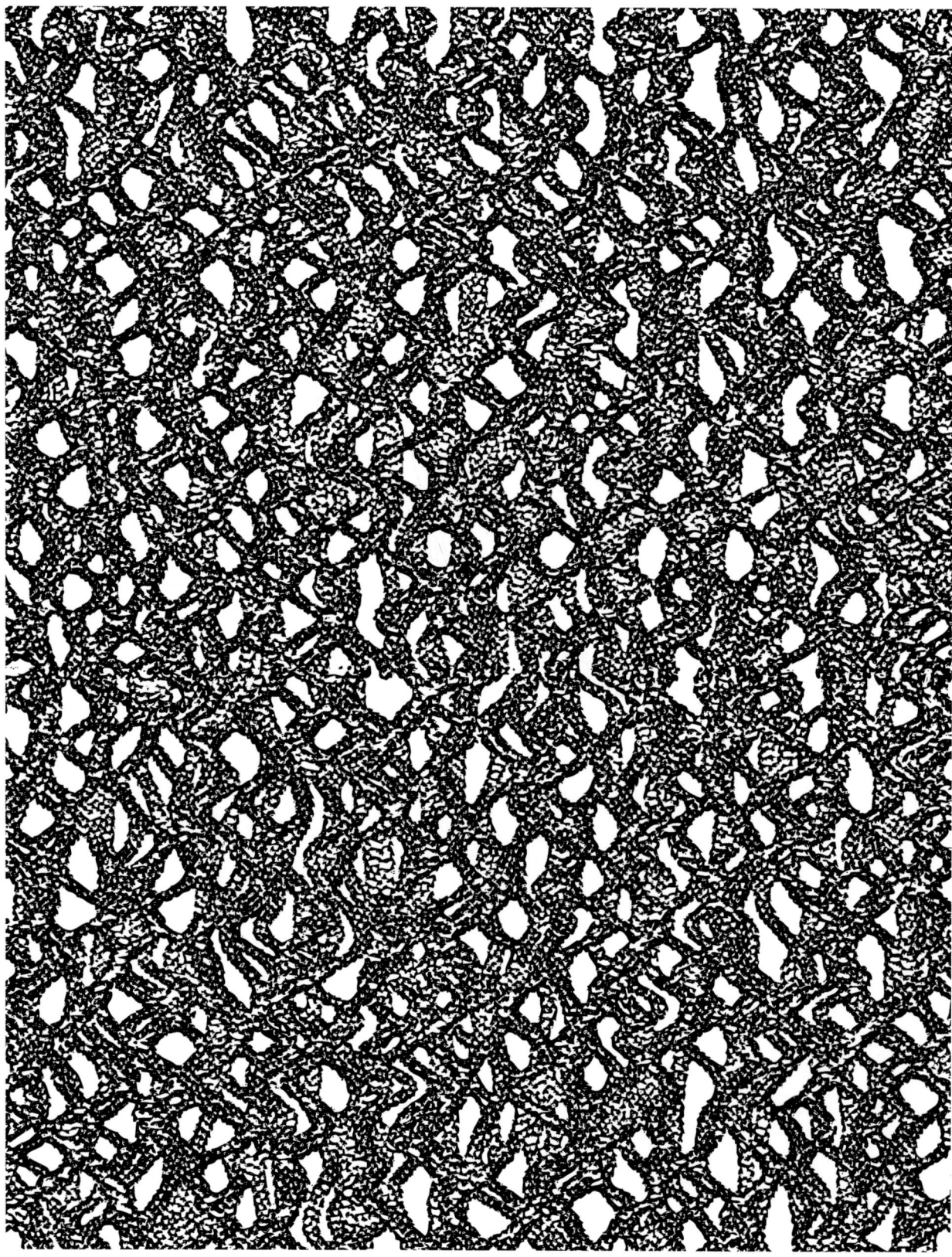

GT0012

pattern size
28 cm x 28 cm

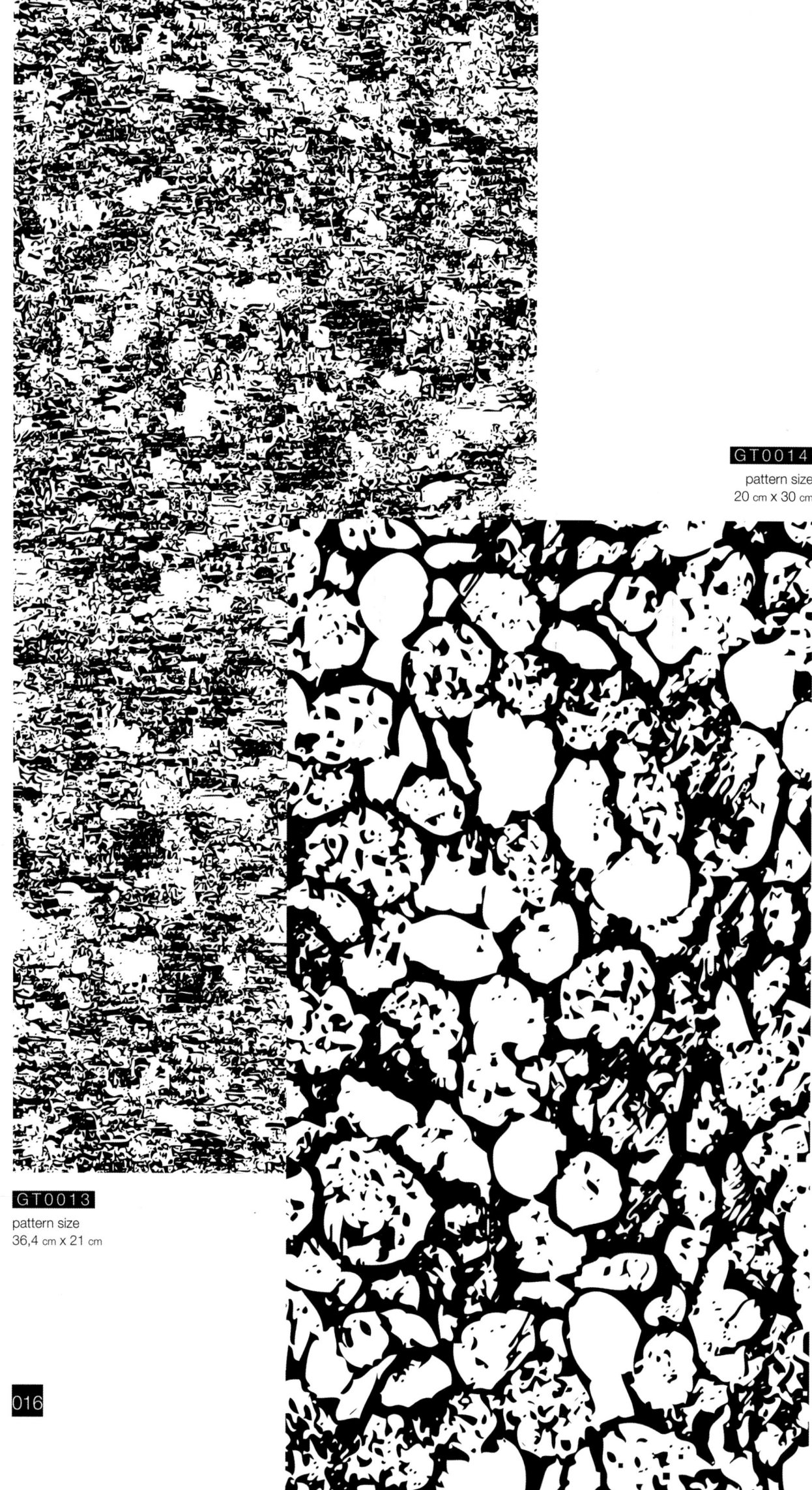

GT0014
pattern size
20 cm x 30 cm

GT0013
pattern size
36,4 cm x 21 cm

016

GT0015
pattern size
36,4 cm x 21 cm

GT0016

pattern size
33 cm x 21 cm

GT0017

pattern size
33 cm x 21 cm

GT0018

pattern size
23,3 cm x 27 cm

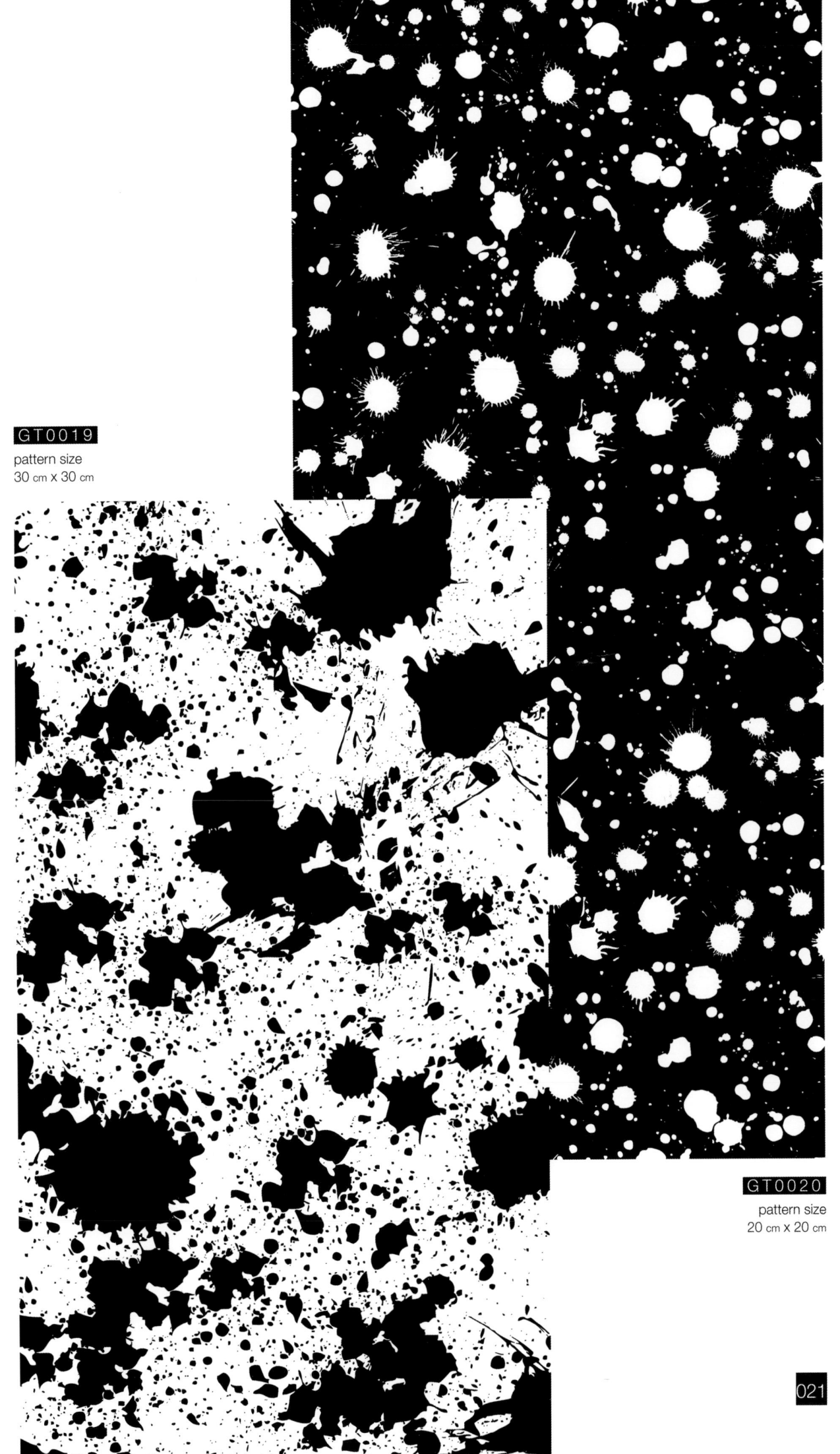

GT0019
pattern size
30 cm x 30 cm

GT0020
pattern size
20 cm x 20 cm

## GT0021
pattern size
24 cm x 40 cm

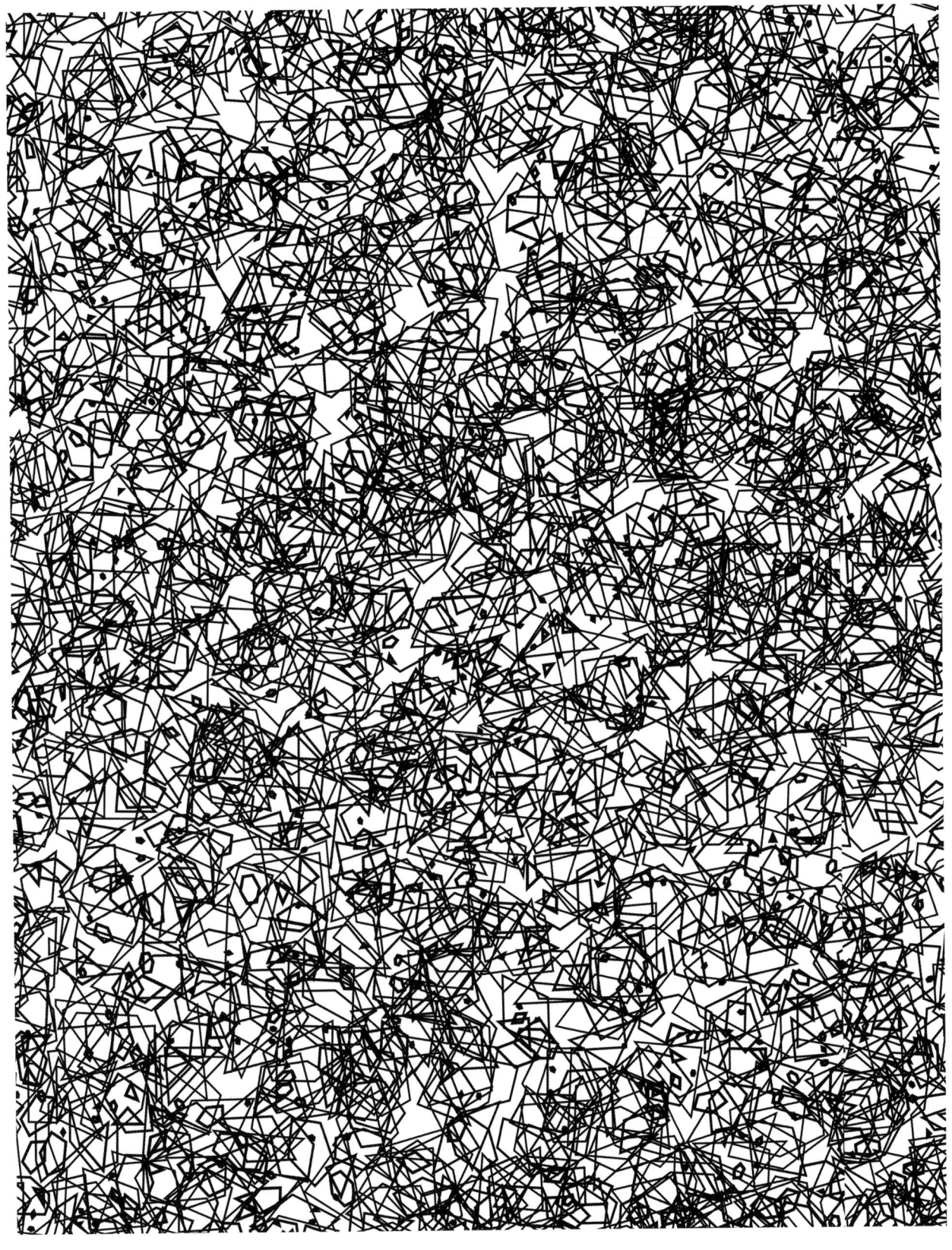

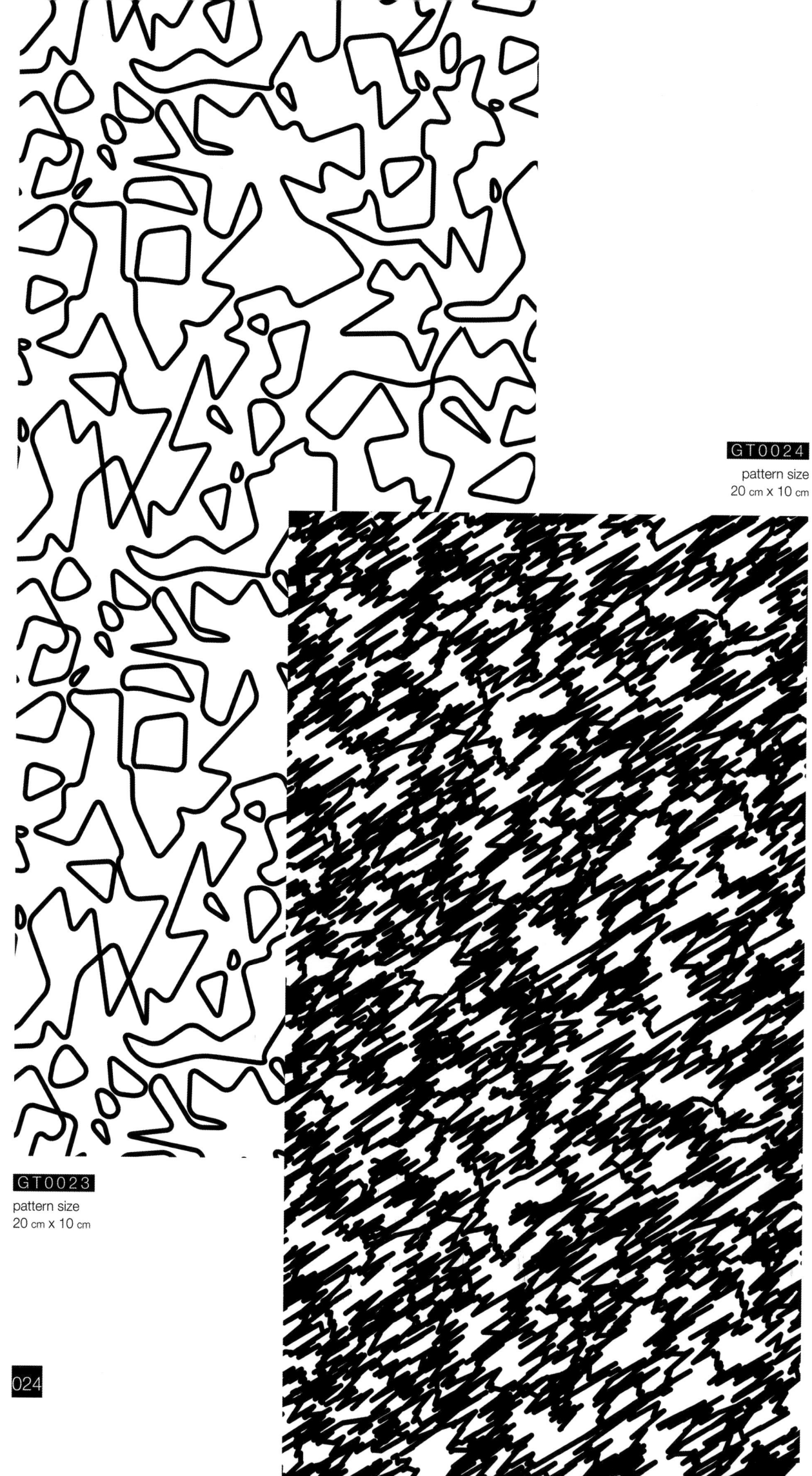

GT0024
pattern size
20 cm x 10 cm

GT0023
pattern size
20 cm x 10 cm

GT0025

pattern size
20 cm x 20 cm

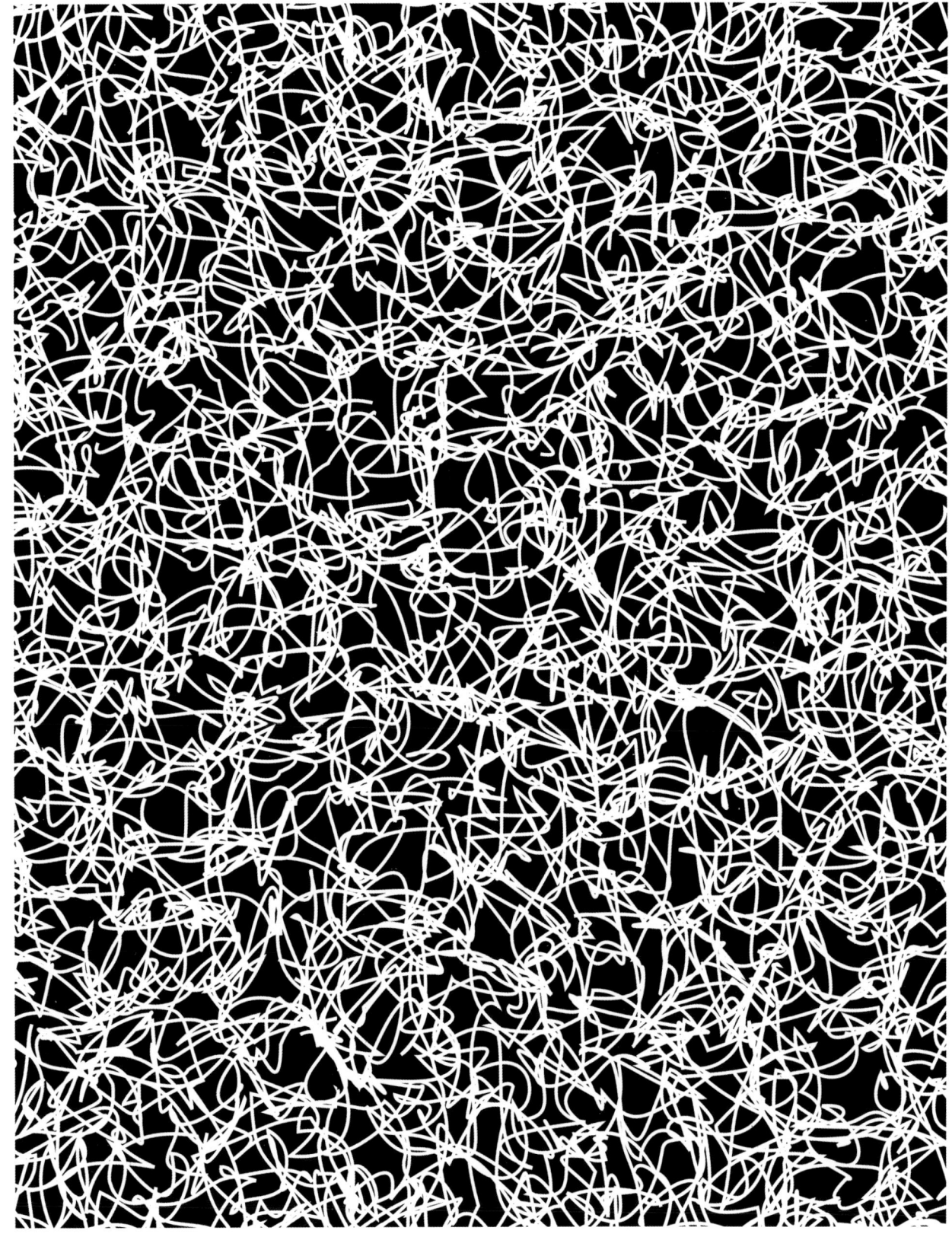

GT0026
pattern size
28,3 cm x 28,3 cm

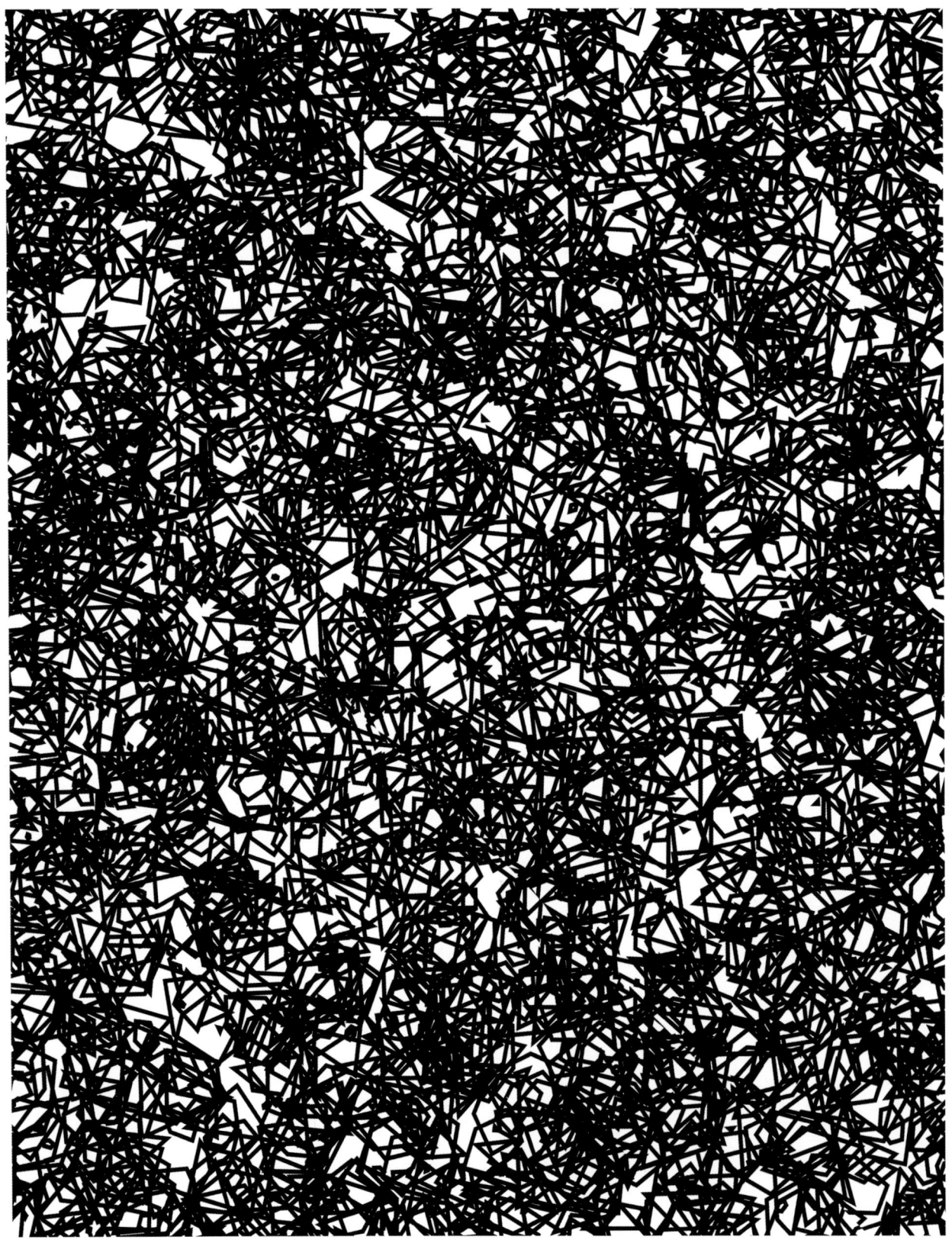

GT0027
pattern size
20 cm x 20 cm

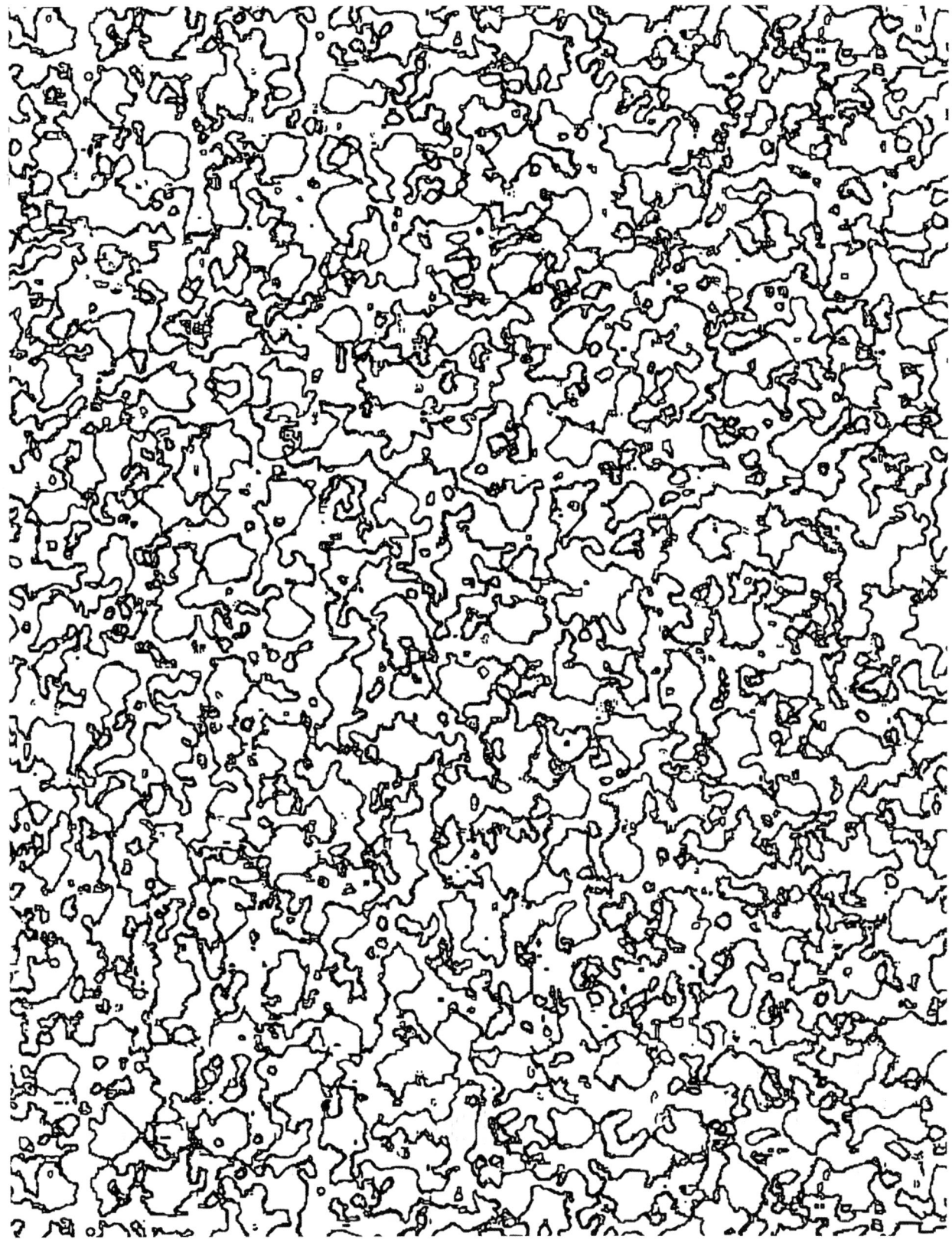

## GT0028

pattern size
20 cm x 20 cm

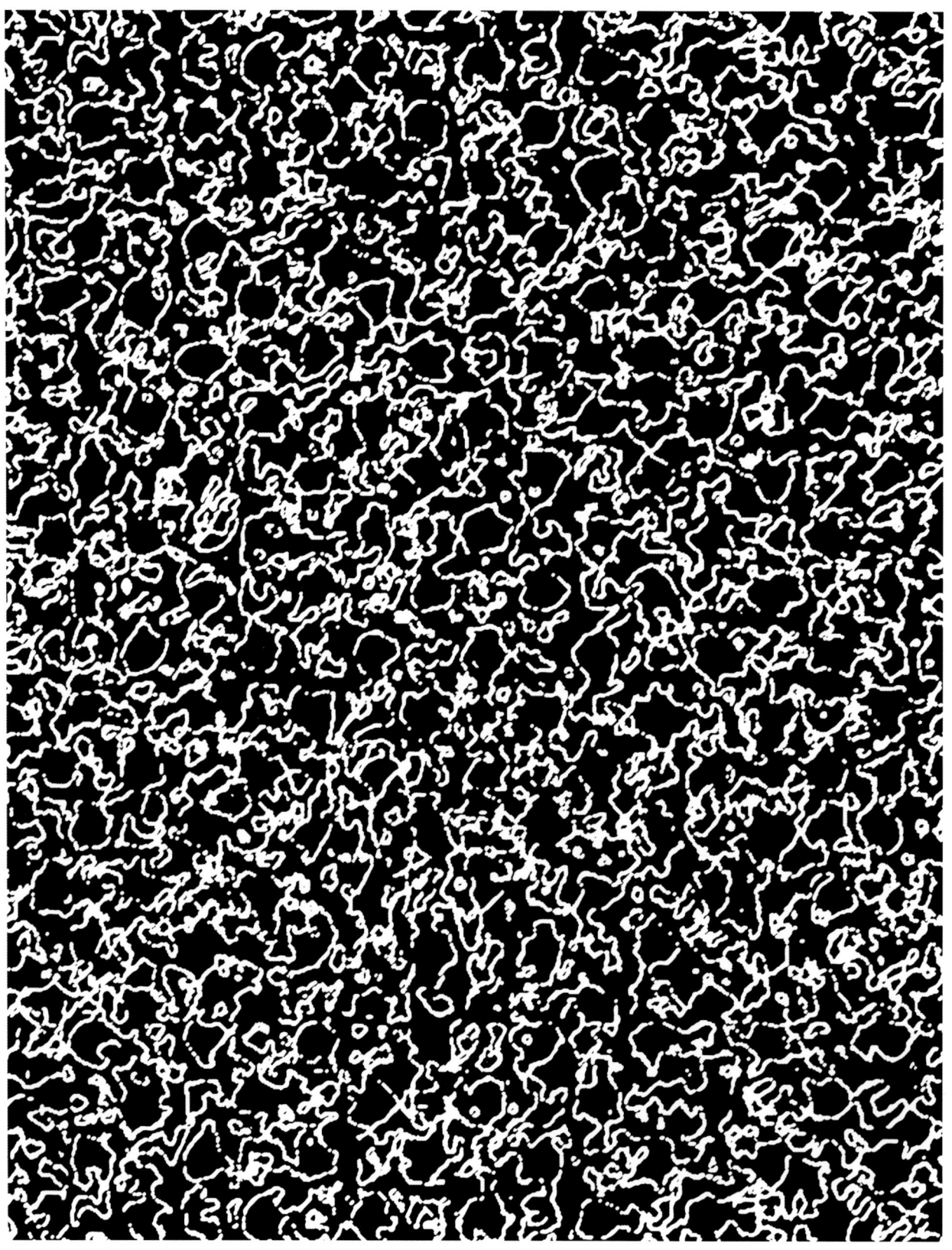

GT0029
pattern size
21 cm x 21 cm

GT0030
pattern size
24 cm x 24 cm

GT0031
pattern size
10 cm x 10 cm

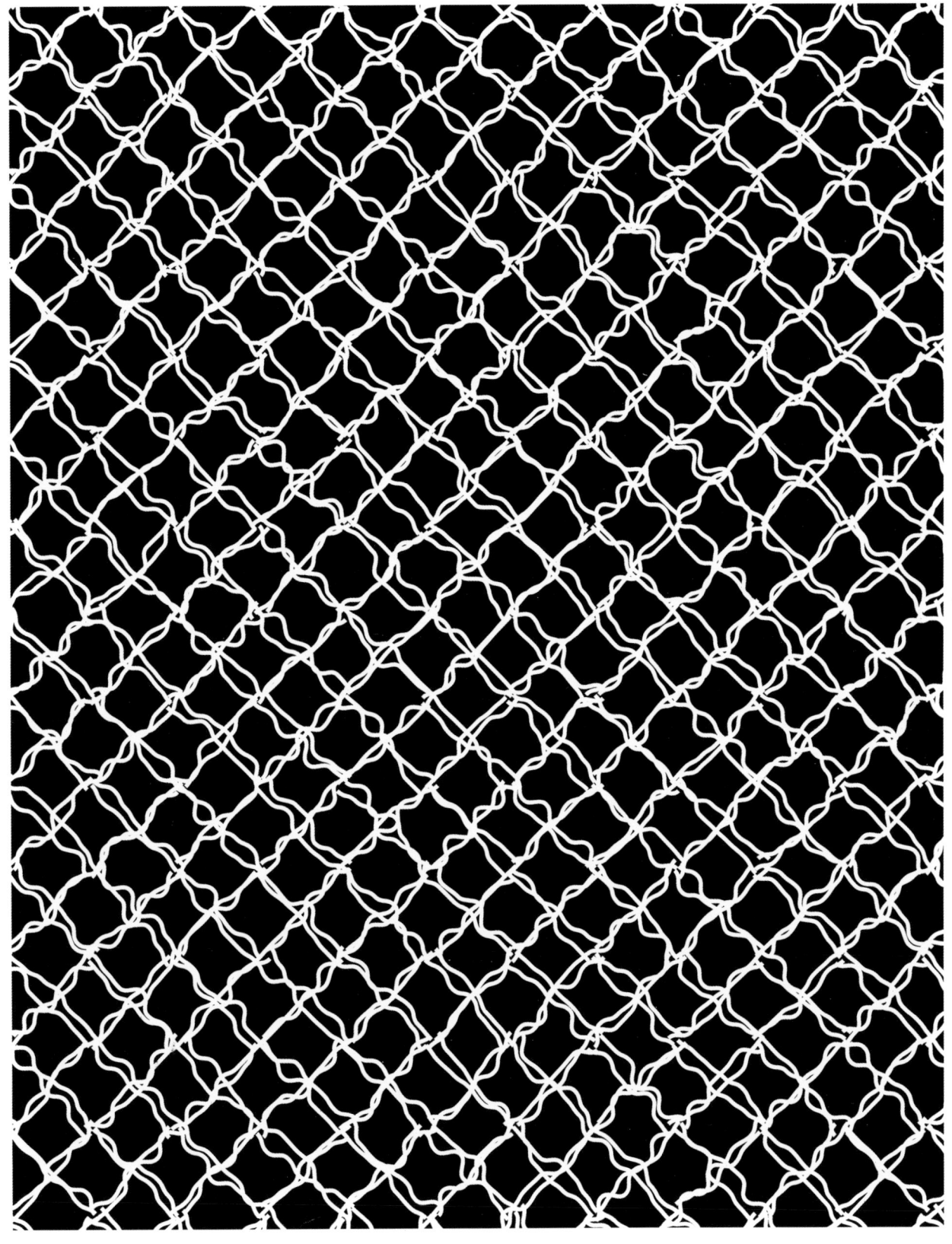

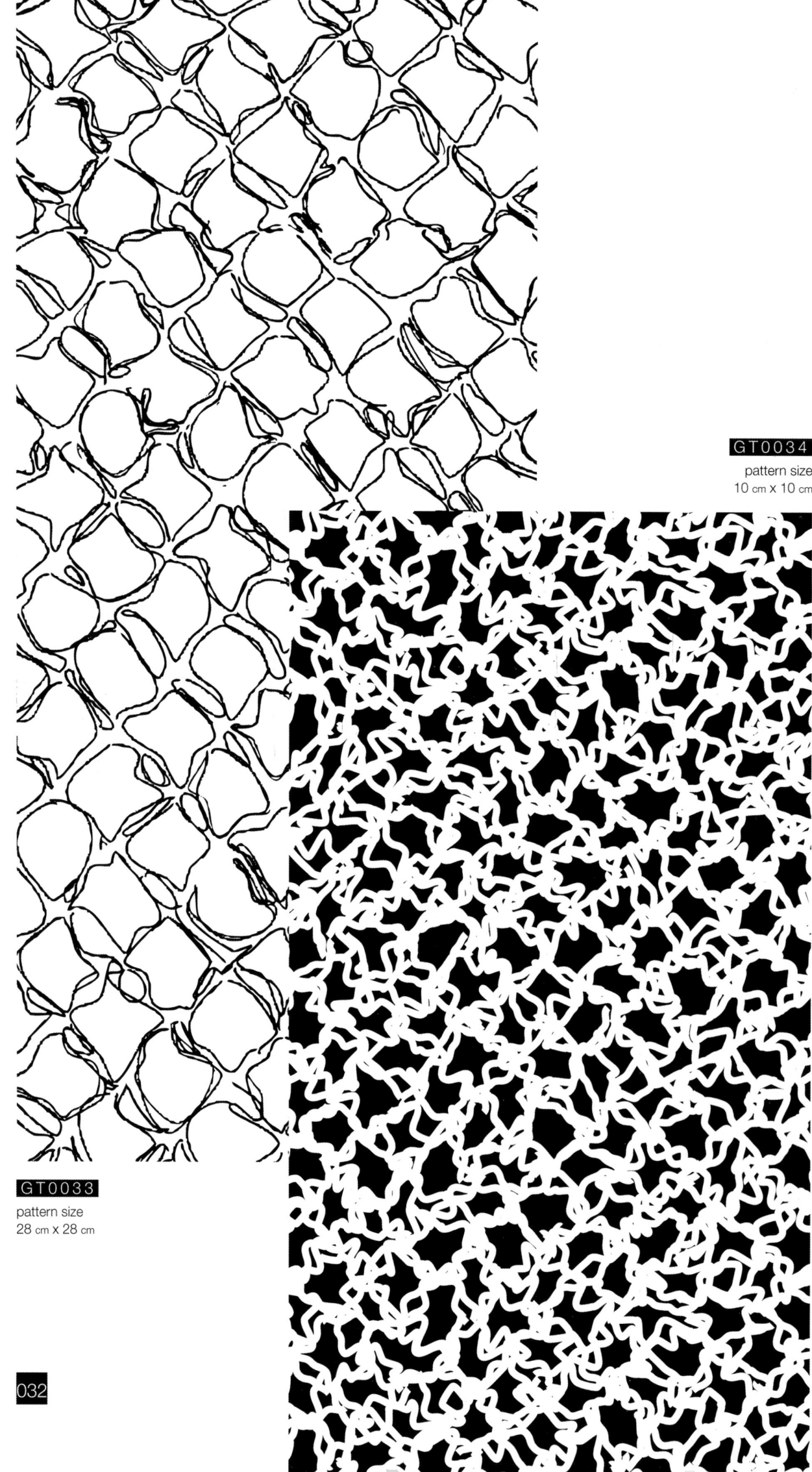

GT0034
pattern size
10 cm x 10 cm

GT0033
pattern size
28 cm x 28 cm

032

GT0035

pattern size
20 cm x 28 cm

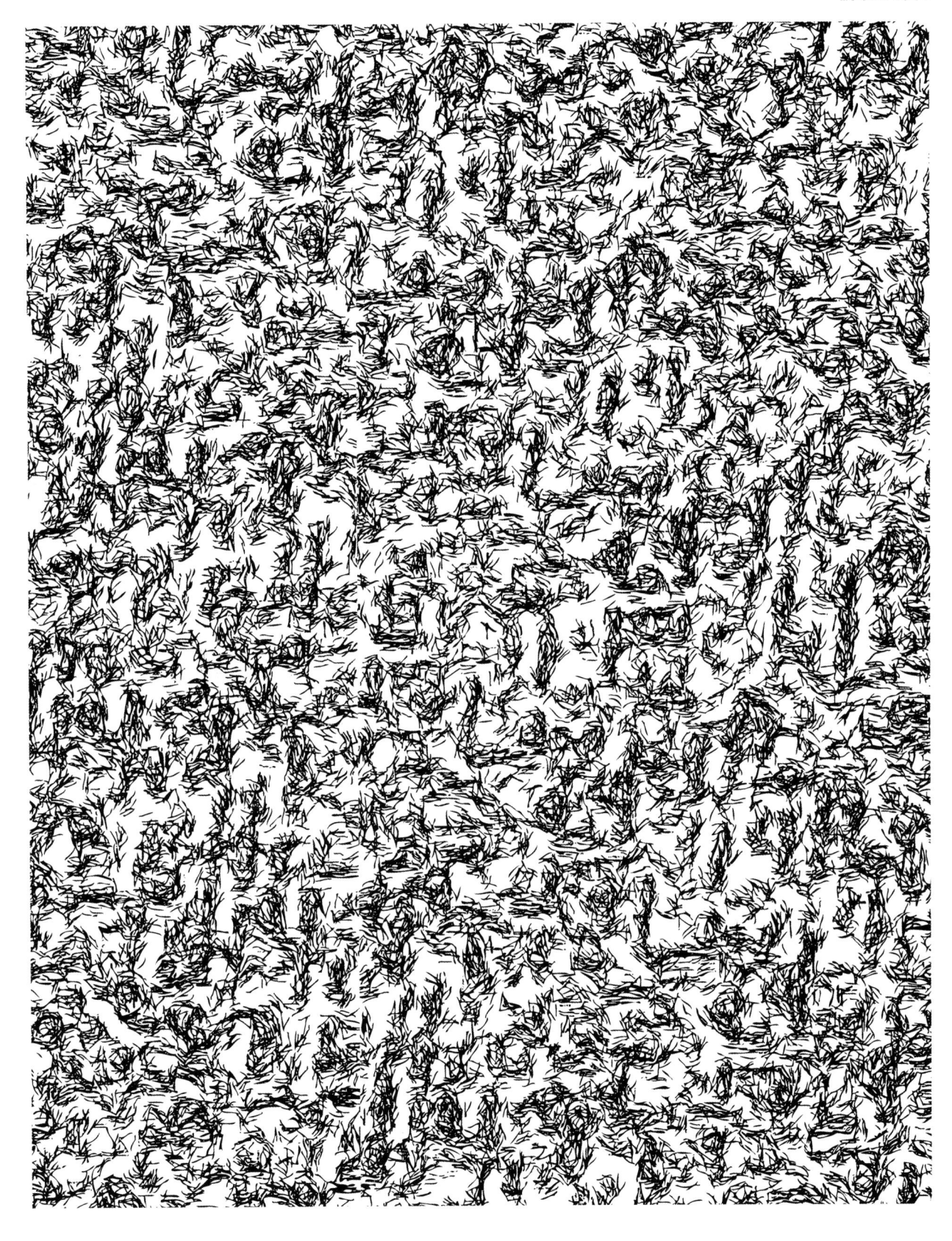

GT0036
pattern size
28 cm x 28 cm

GT0038

pattern size
21 cm x 23,3 cm

GT0039

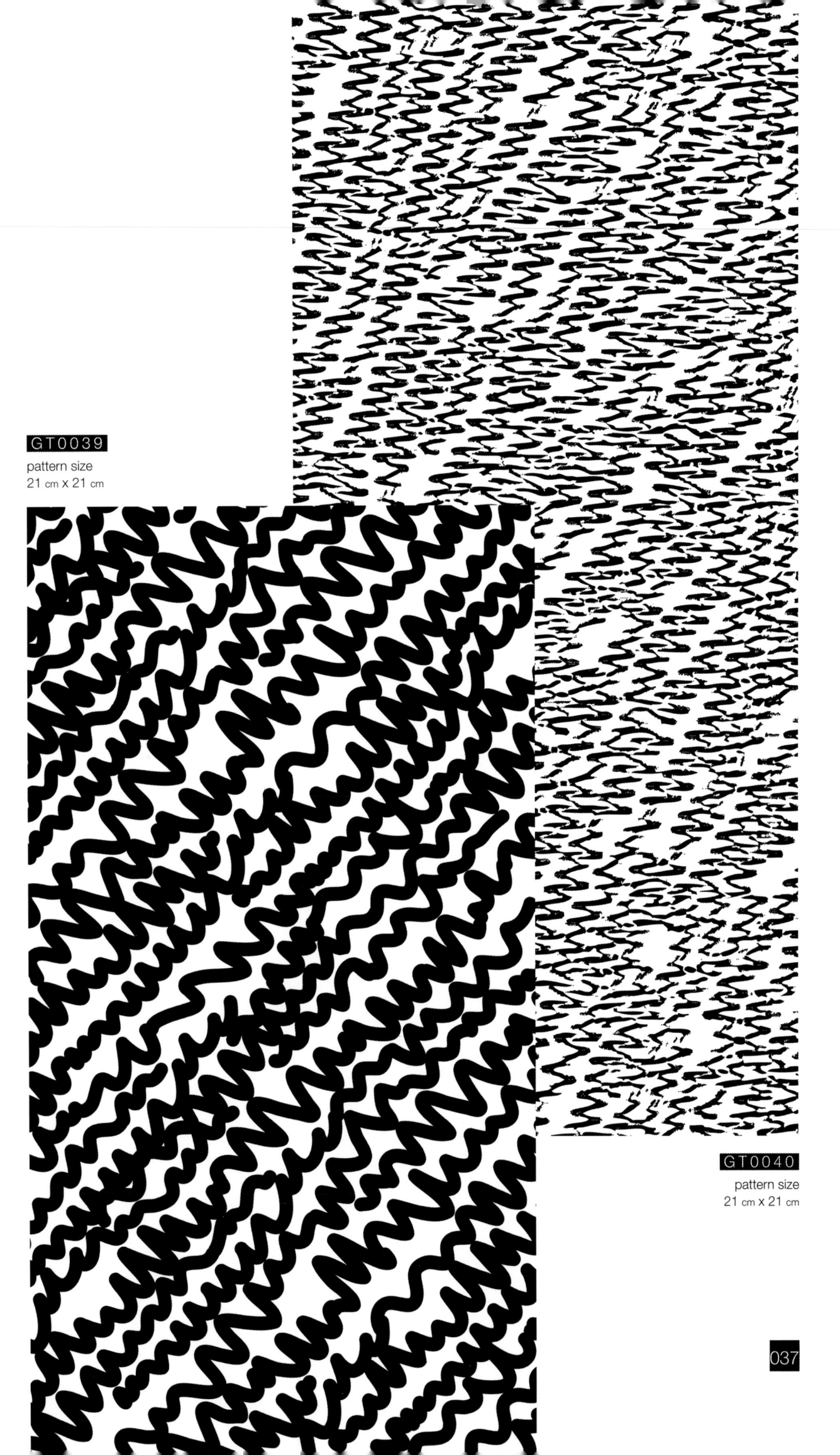

pattern size
21 cm x 21 cm

GT0040

pattern size
21 cm x 21 cm

037

GT0041

pattern size
21 cm x 21 cm

GT0042
pattern size
40 cm x 40 cm

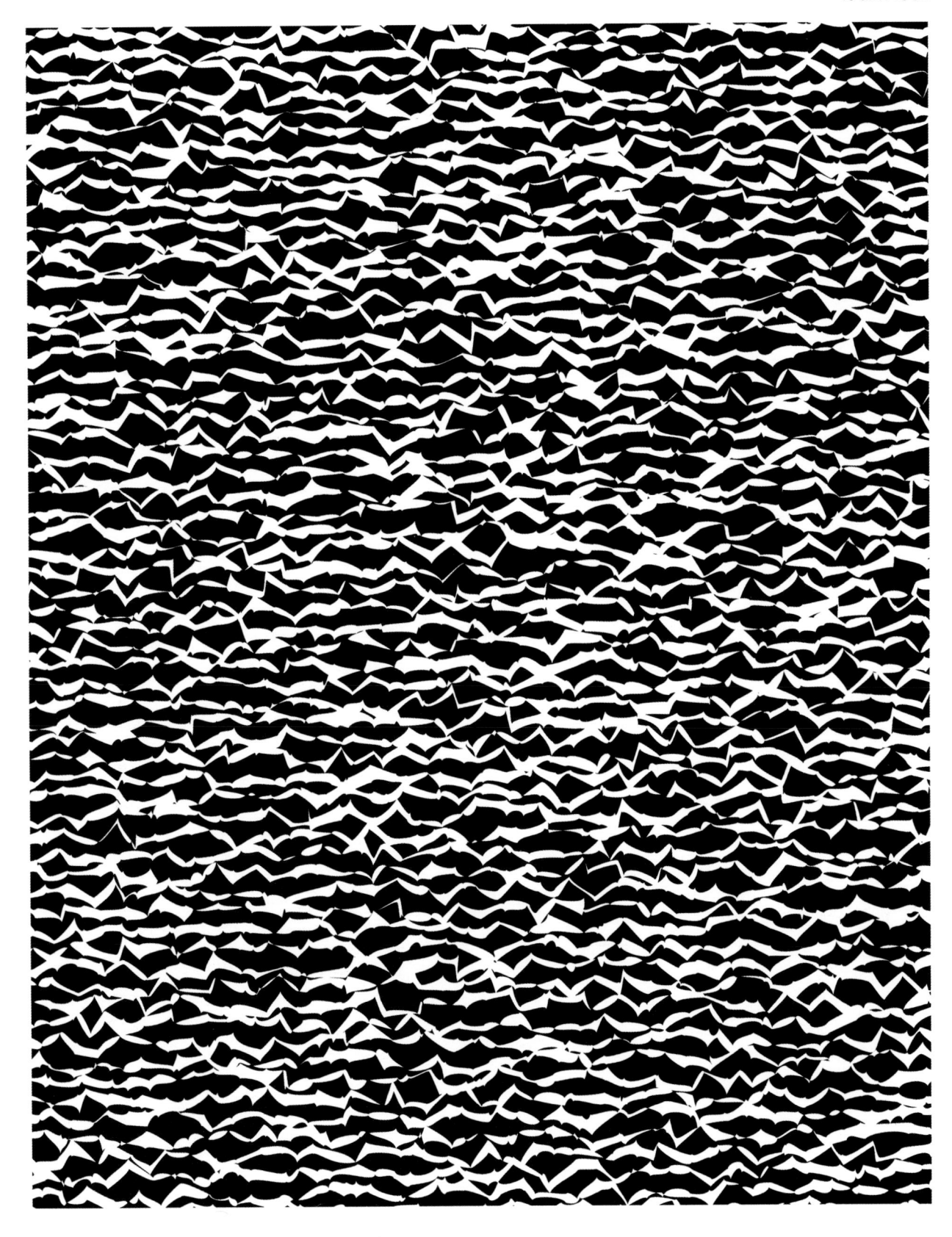

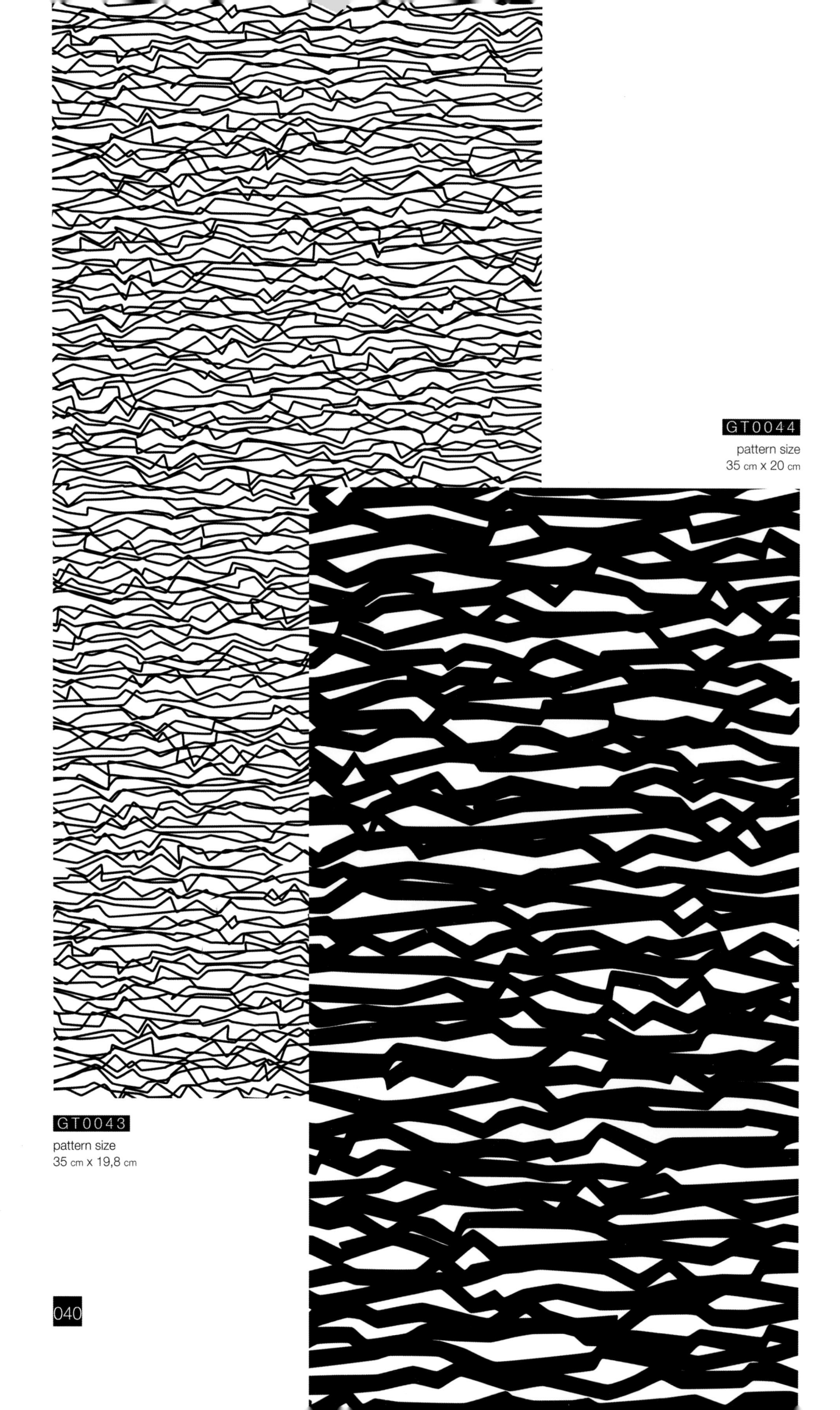

GT0044
pattern size
35 cm x 20 cm

GT0043
pattern size
35 cm x 19,8 cm

040

GT0045

pattern size
40 cm x 40 cm

GT0046

pattern size
27 cm x 34 cm

GT0047
pattern size
30 cm x 27 cm

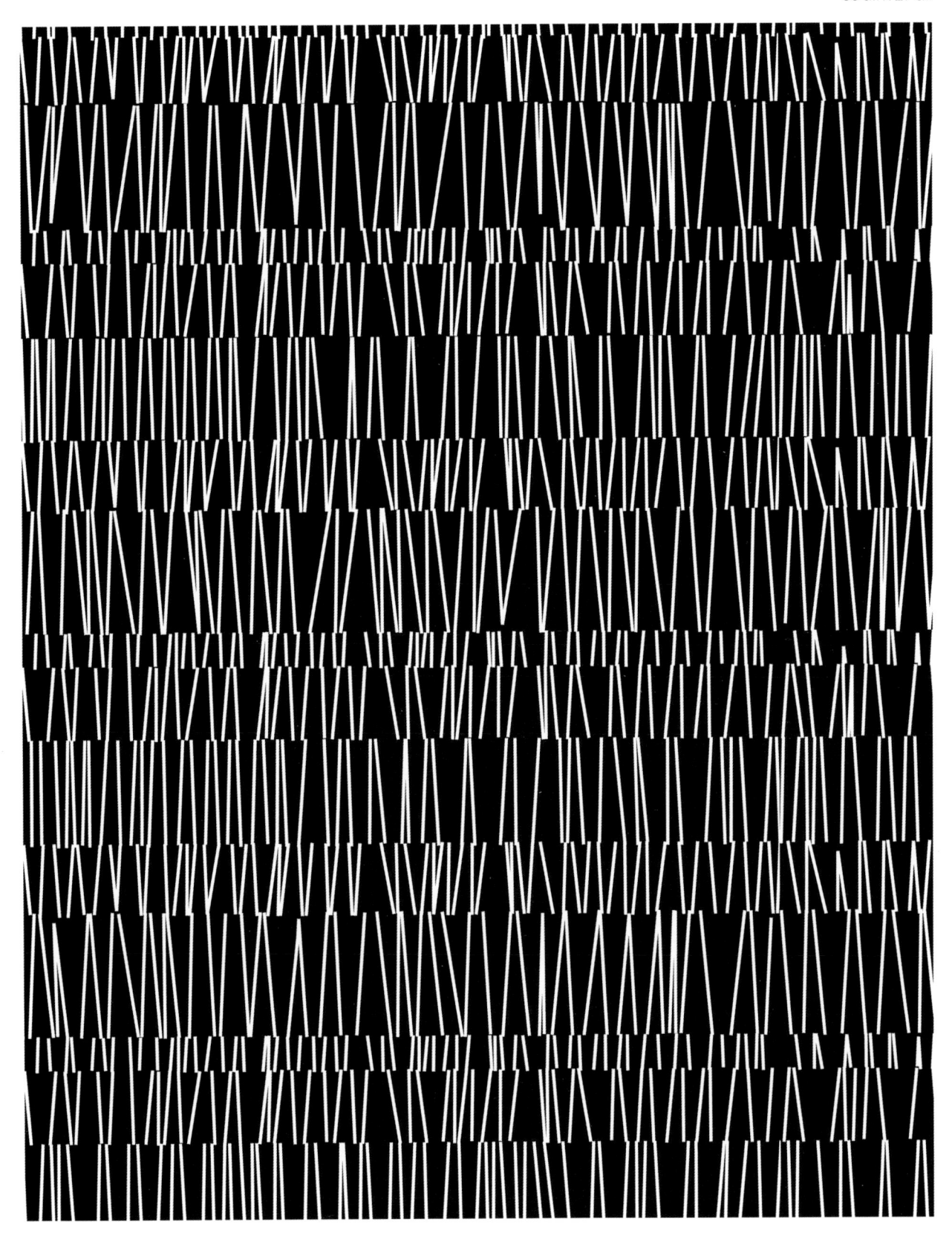

GT0048
pattern size
28,8 cm x 28,8 cm

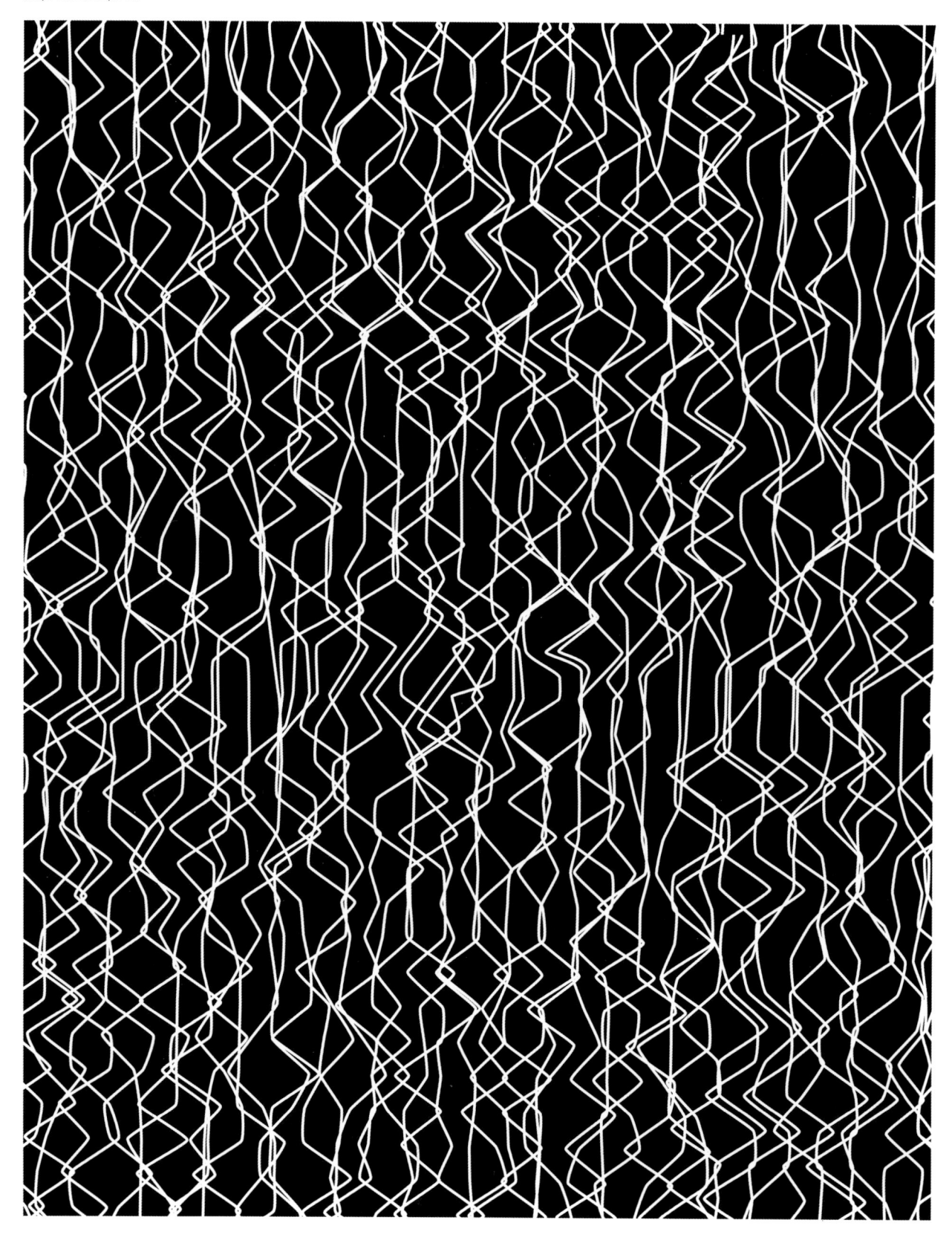

GT0049
pattern size
14,25 cm x 57 cm

GT0050
pattern size
40 cm x 40 cm

045

GT0051
pattern size
40 cm x 40 cm

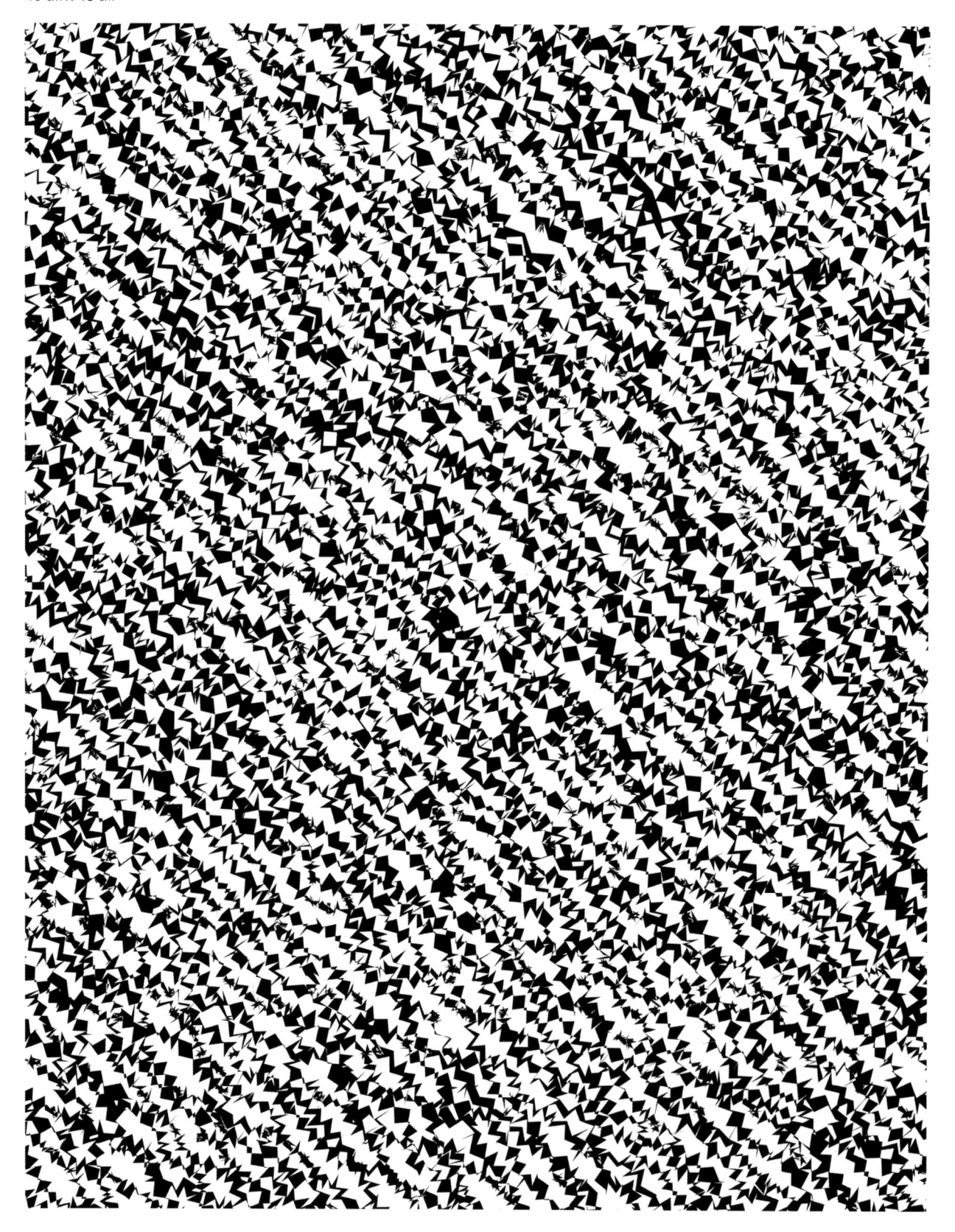

046

GT0052
pattern size
20 cm x 20 cm

047

GT0054
pattern size
25 cm x 25 cm

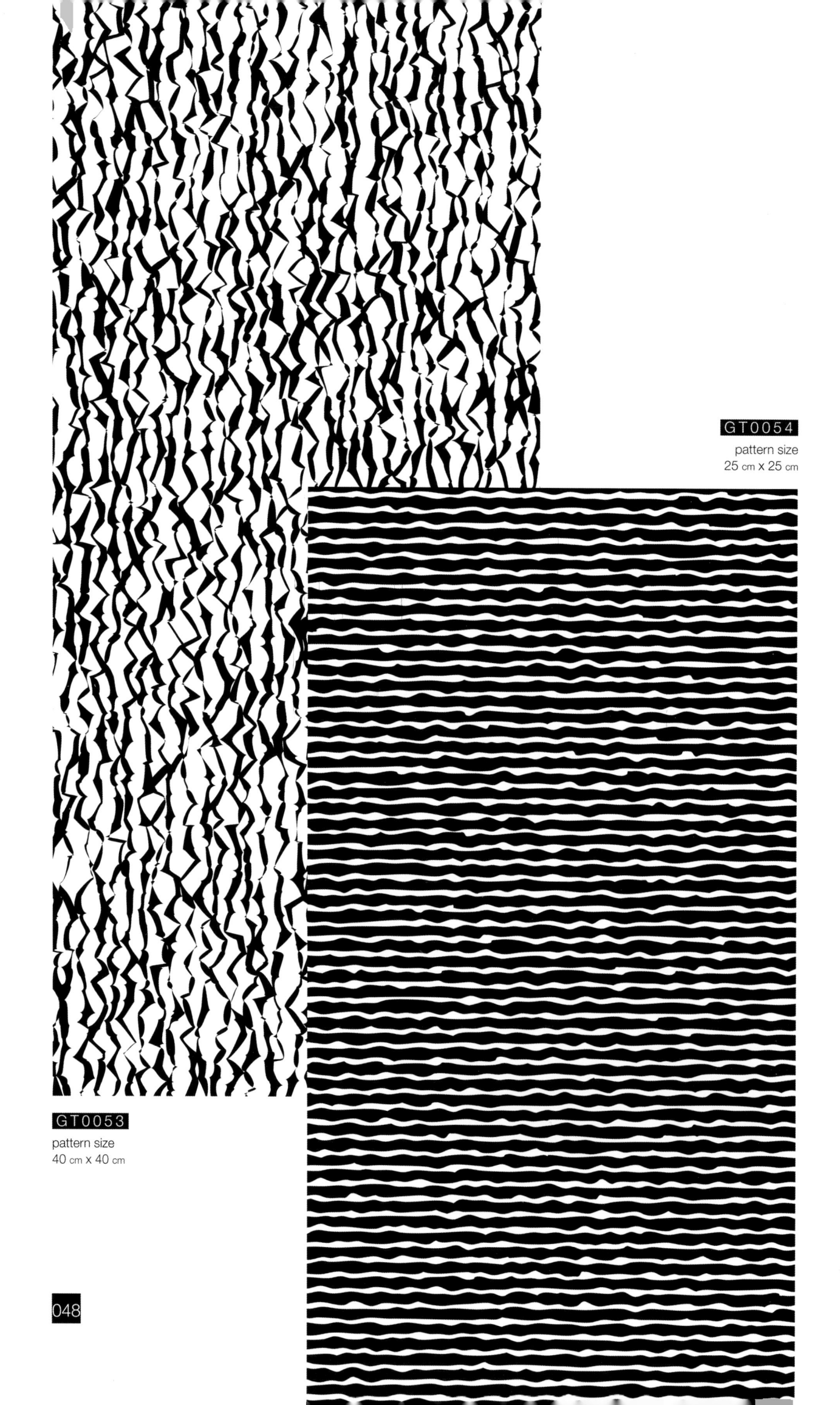

GT0053
pattern size
40 cm x 40 cm

048

GT0055

pattern size
42 cm x 42 cm

GT0056
pattern size
40 cm x 40 cm

GT0057

pattern size
30 cm x 30 cm

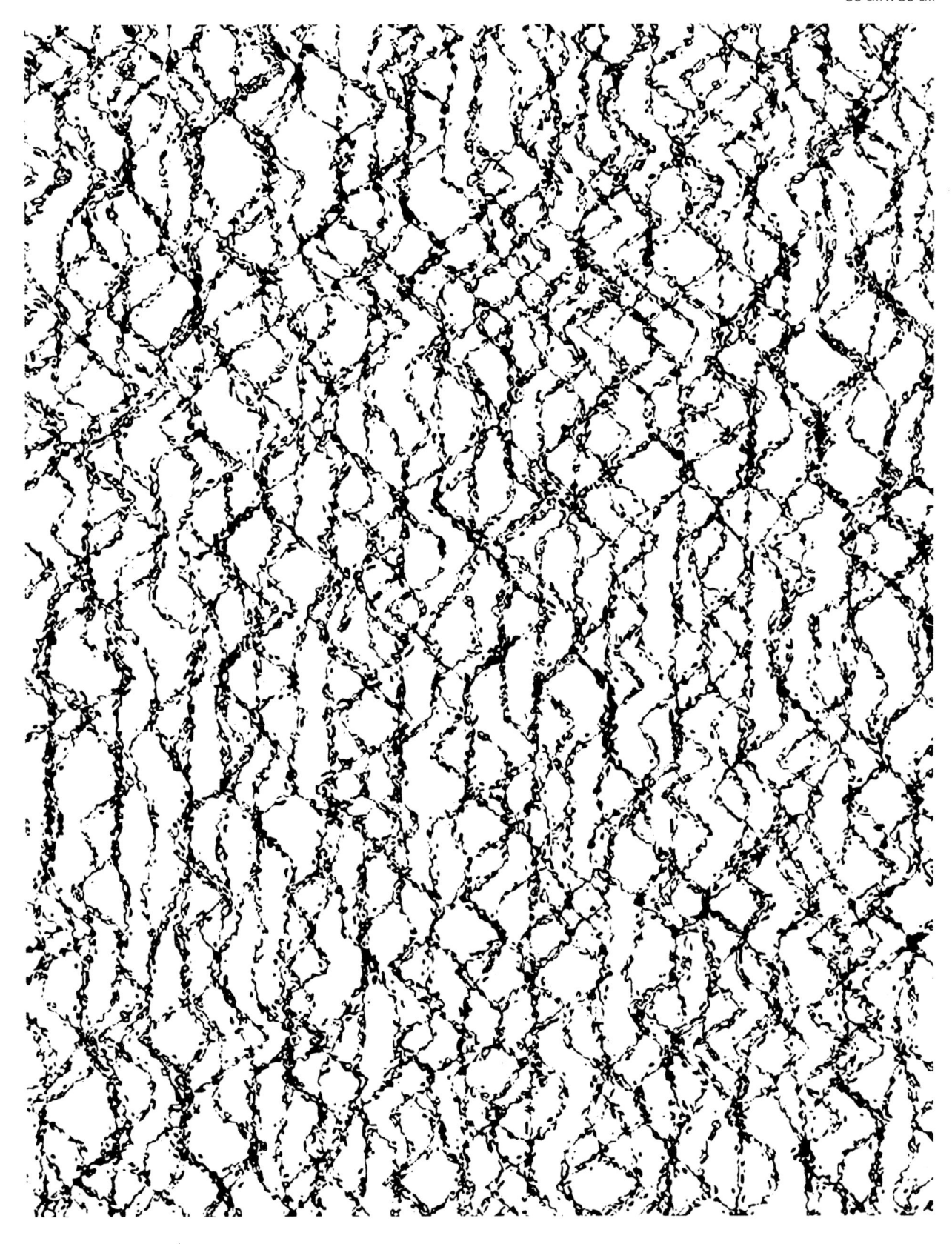

GT0058

pattern size
8 cm x 8 cm

GT0059
pattern size
21 cm x 21 cm

GT0060
pattern size
8 cm x 8 cm

053

GT0061

pattern size
20 cm x 20 cm

GT0062

pattern size
39,6 cm x 39,6 cm

055

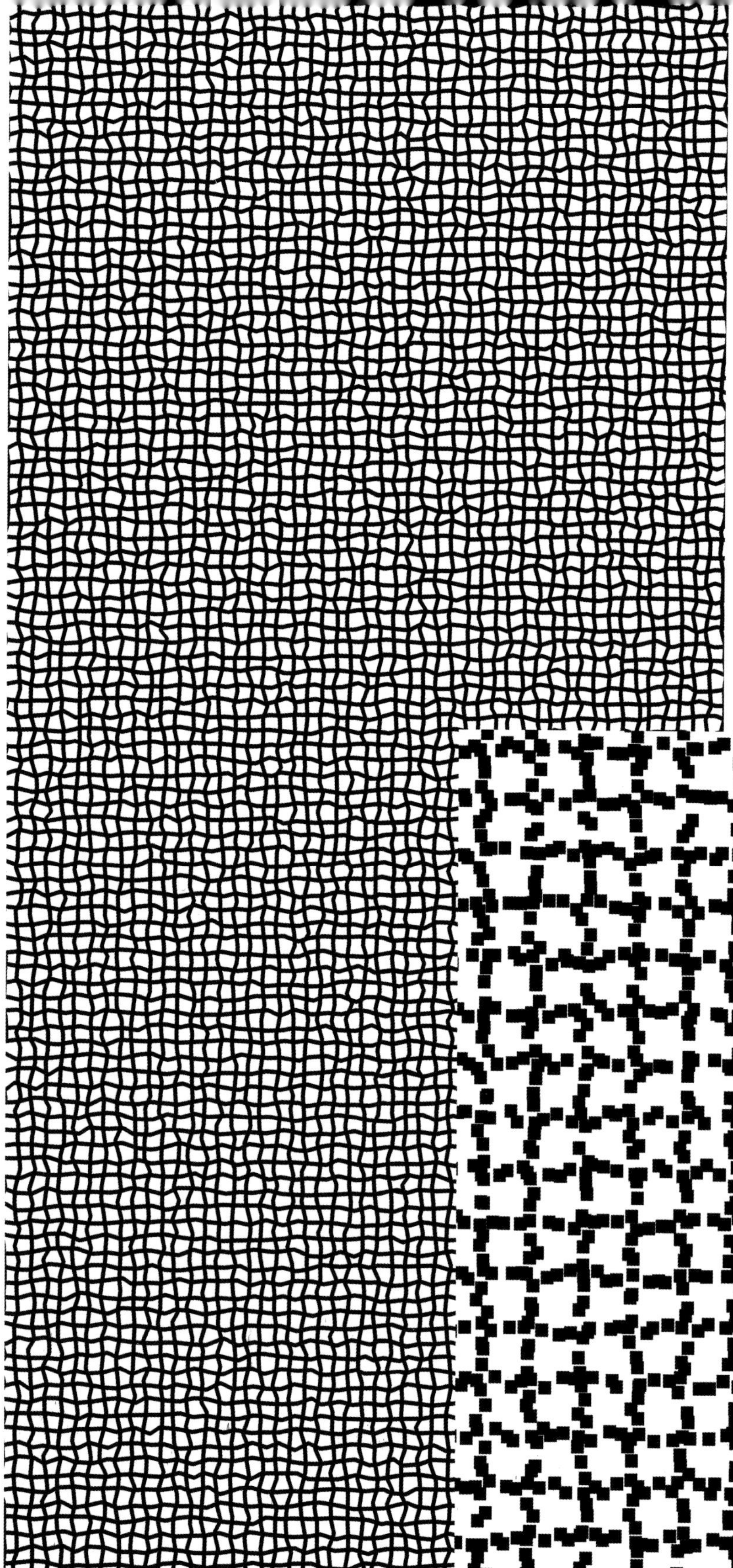

GT0064
pattern size
38,2 cm x 38,2 cm

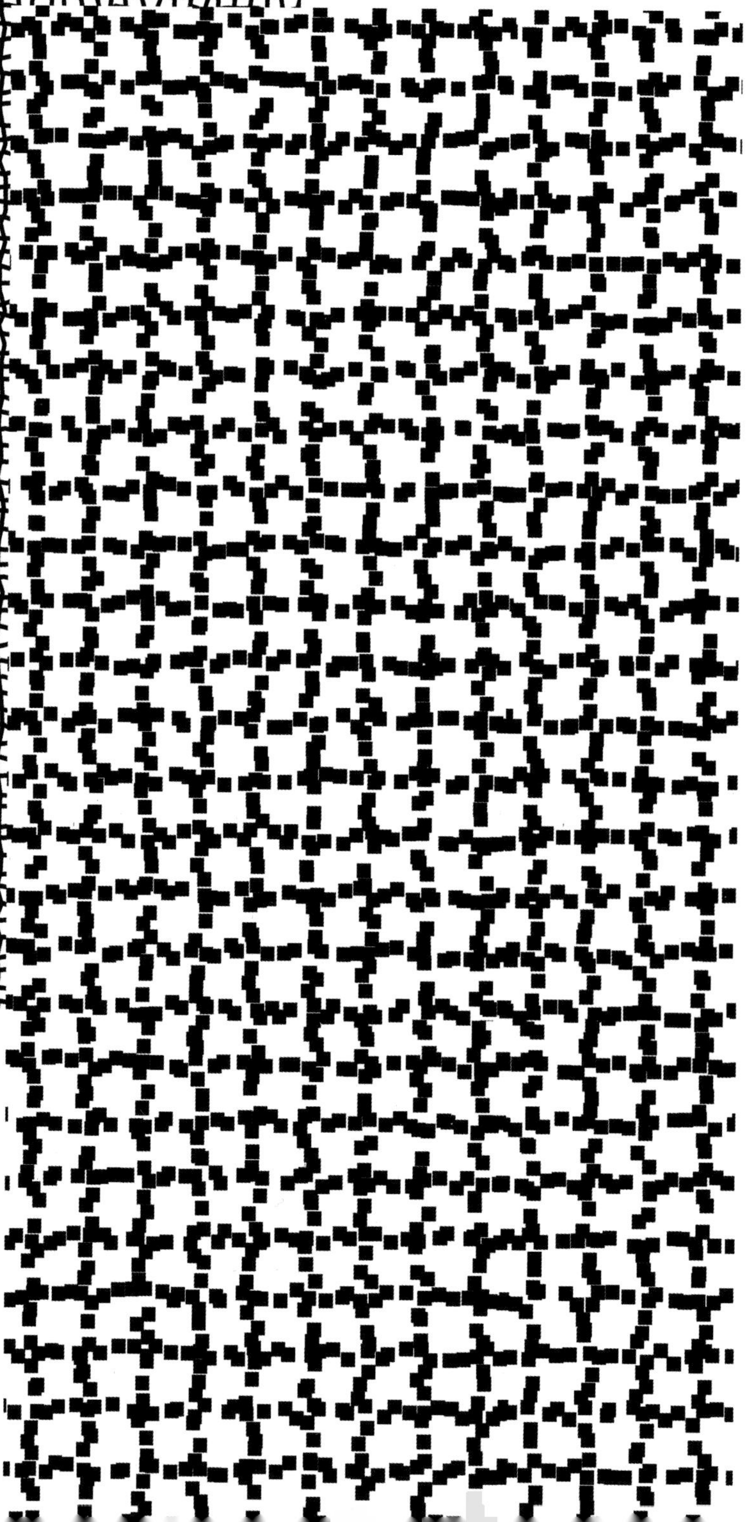

GT0063
pattern size
40 cm x 40 cm

GT0065

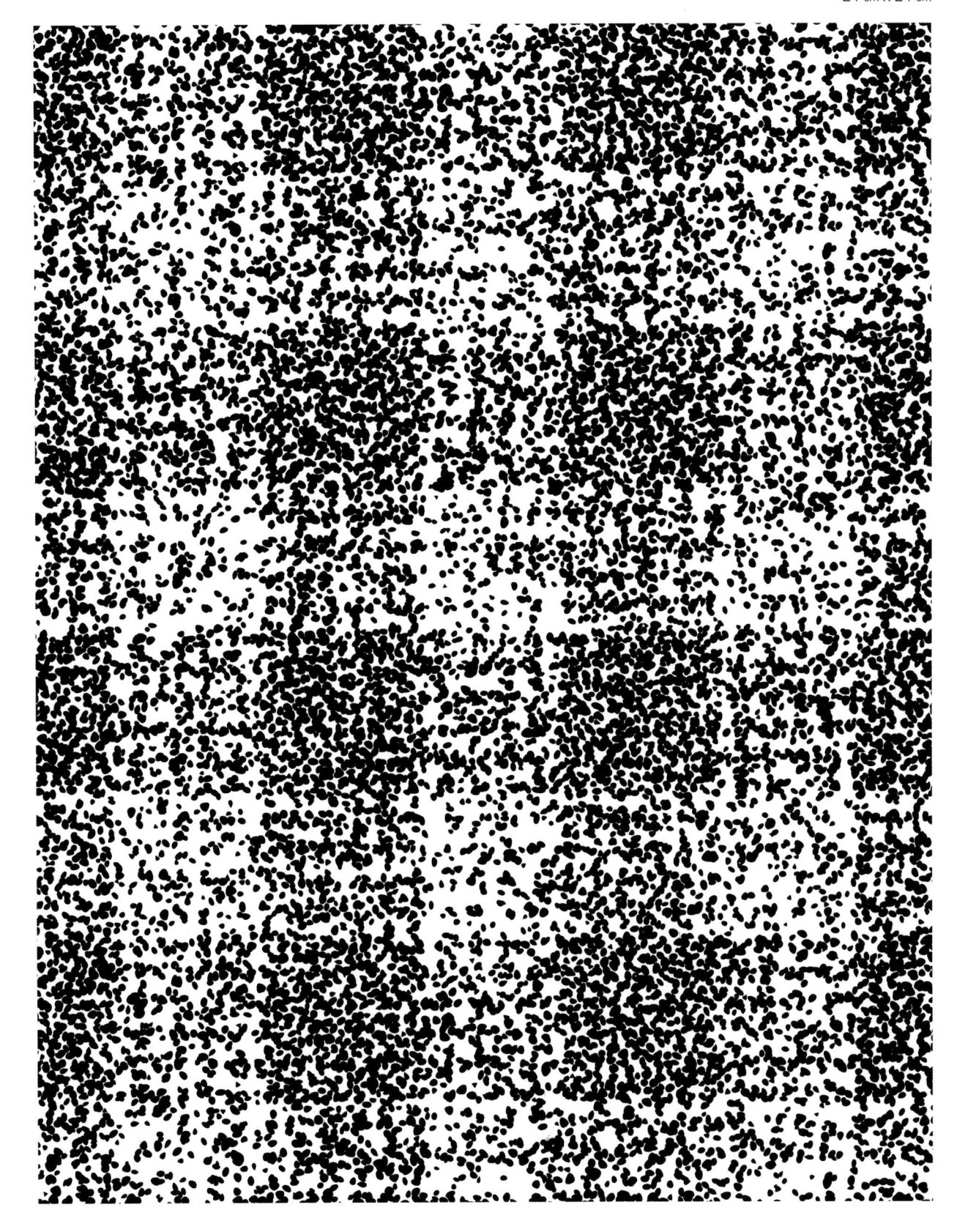

pattern size
24 cm x 24 cm

057

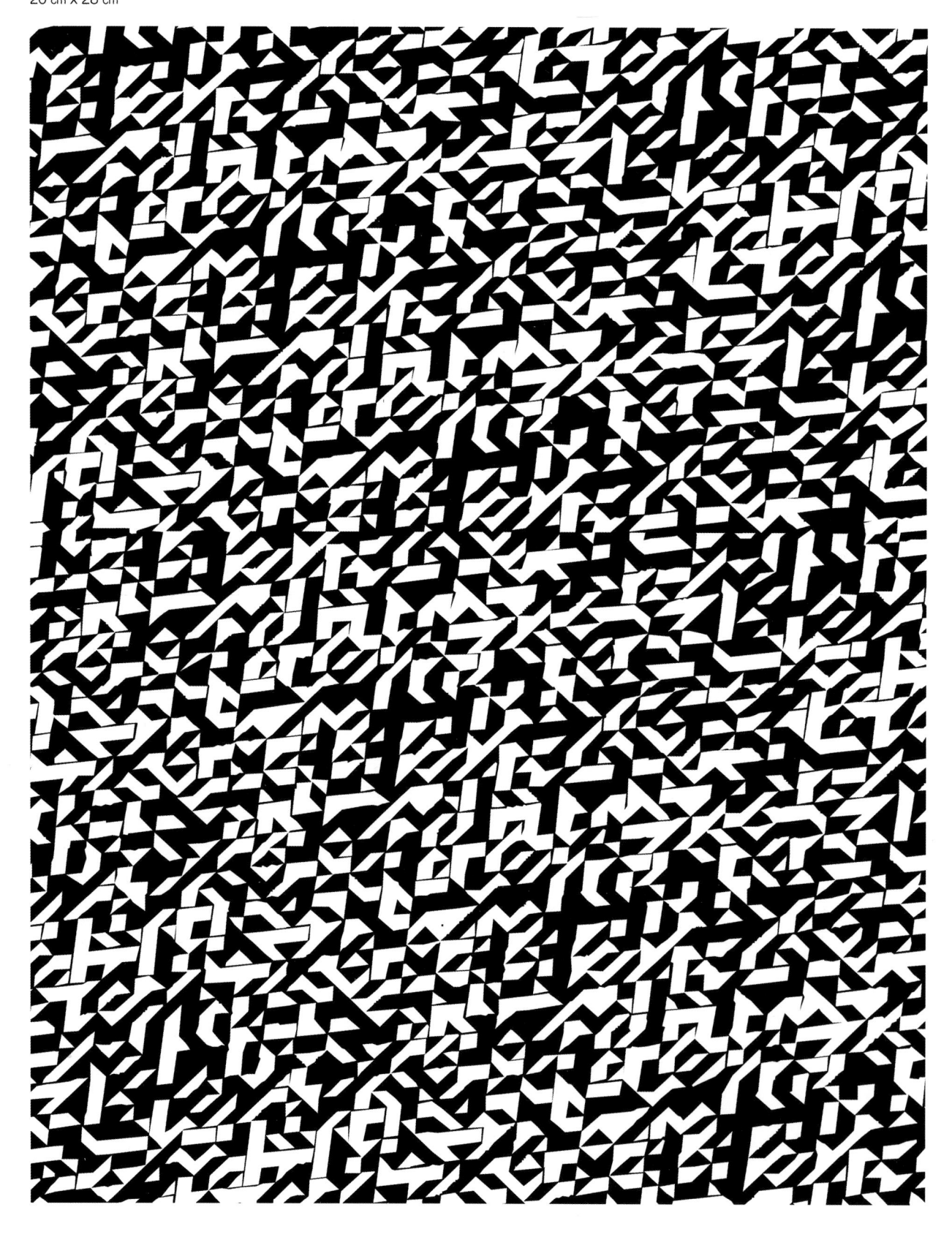

GT0066
pattern size
20 cm x 28 cm

GT0067
pattern size
15 cm x 15 cm

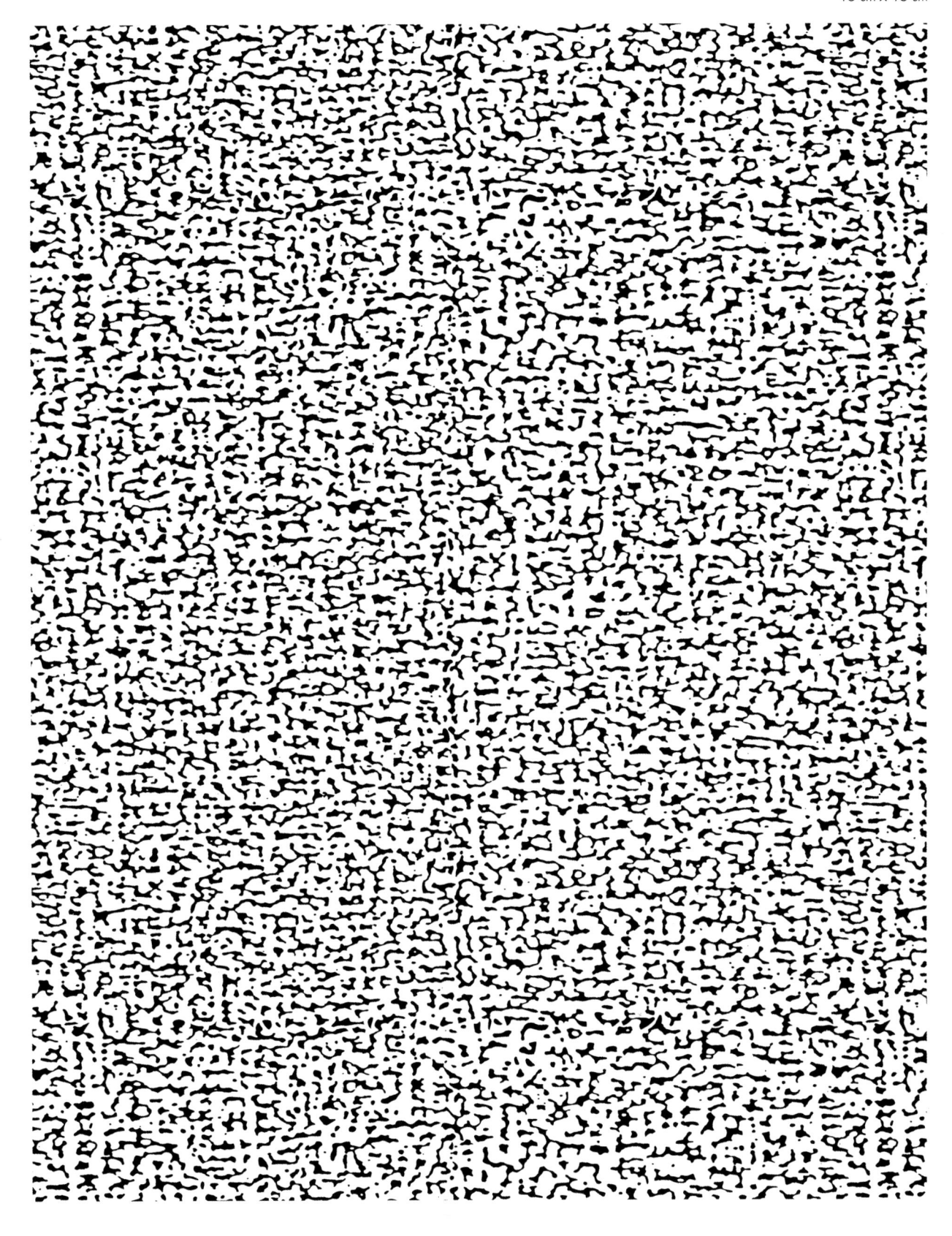

GT0068
pattern size
24,2 cm x 24,2 cm

060

GT0069
pattern size
8 cm x 8 cm

GT0070
pattern size
12,5 cm x 12,5 cm

061

GT0071

pattern size
24 cm x 24 cm

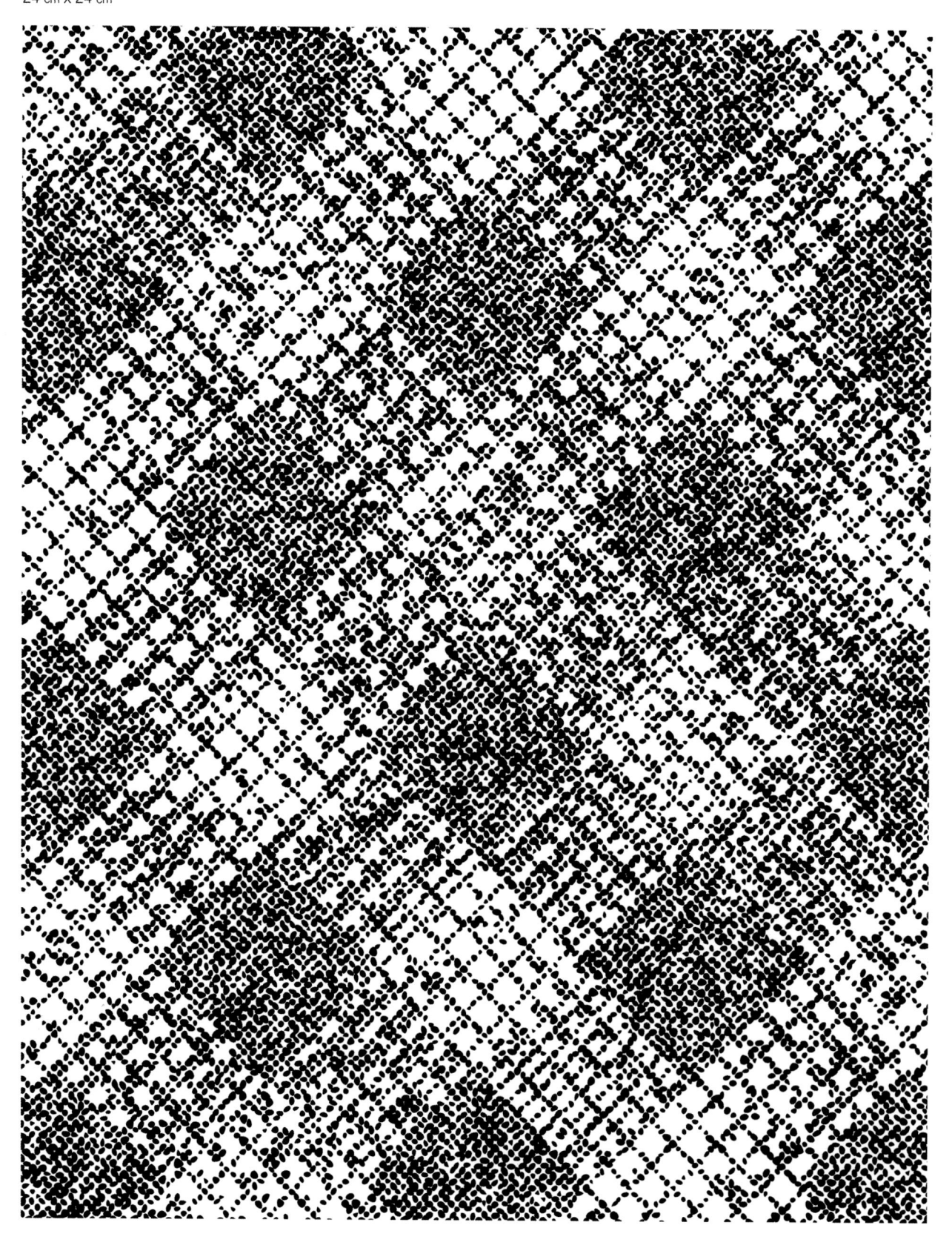

GT0072

pattern size
30 cm x 18 cm

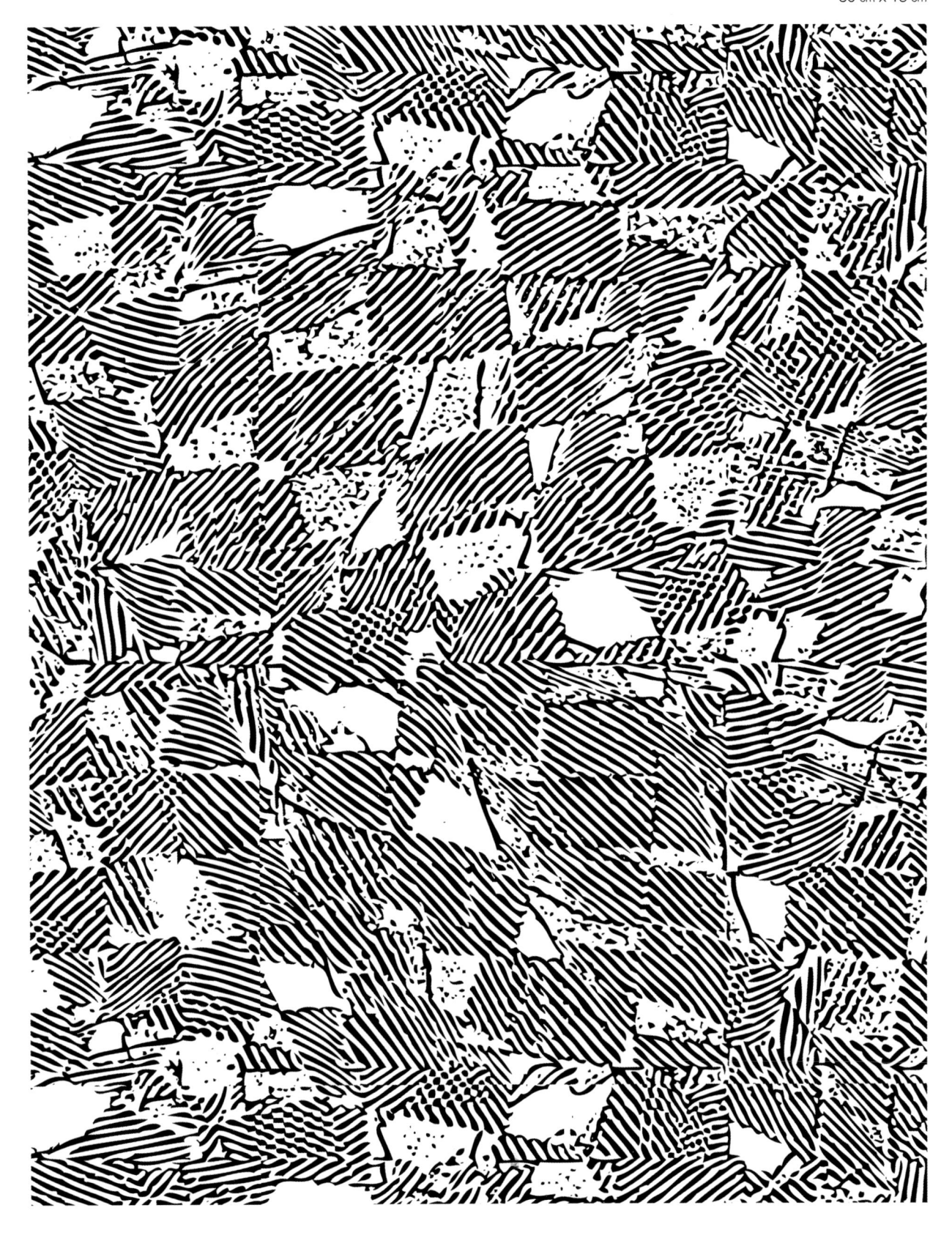

GT0074
pattern size
8 cm x 8 cm

GT0073
pattern size
22 cm x 22 cm

GT0075
pattern size
11 cm x 11 cm

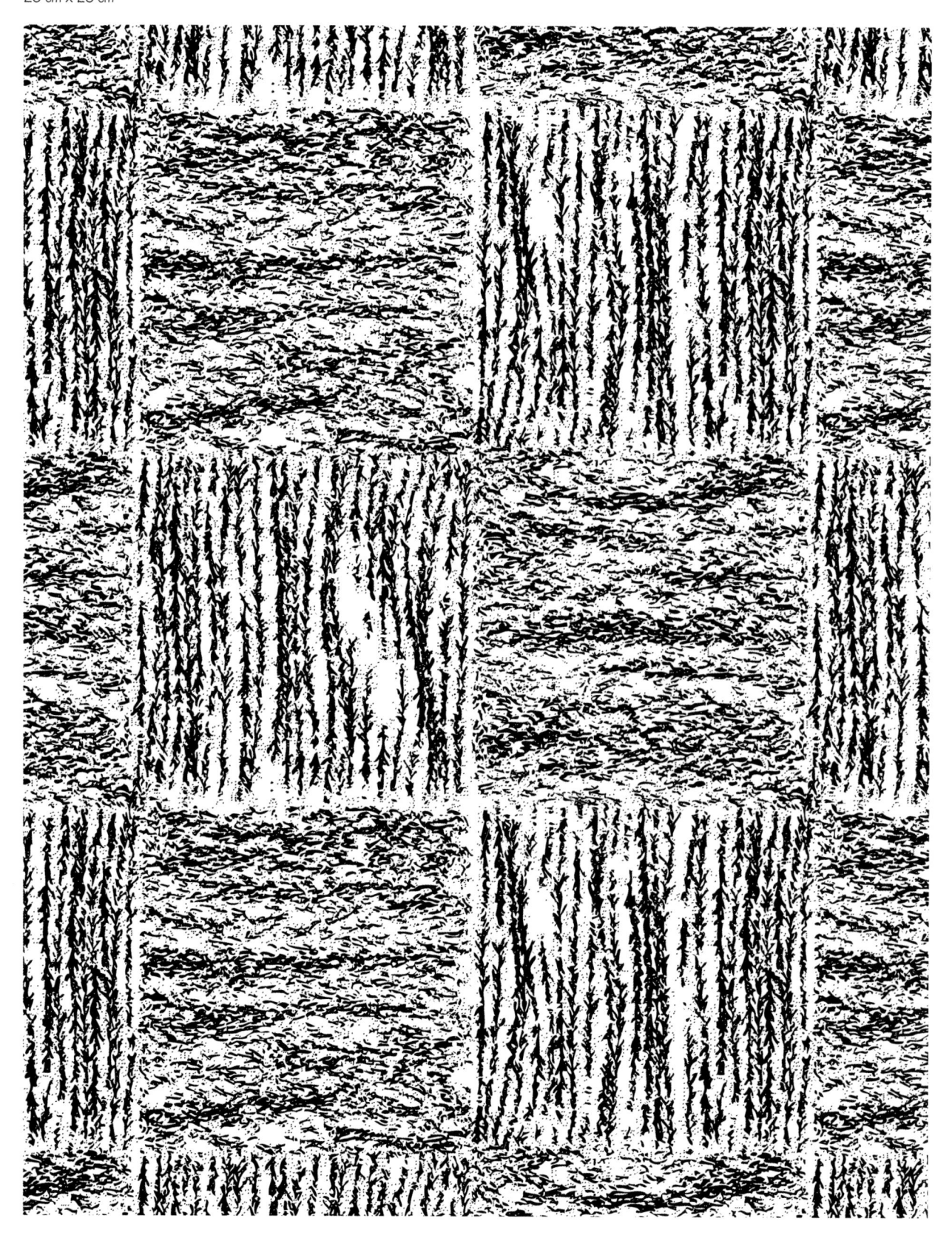

GT0076
pattern size
25 cm x 25 cm

GT0077

pattern size
15 cm x 20 cm

GT0078
pattern size
20 cm x 20 cm

GT0079
pattern size
8 cm x 8 cm

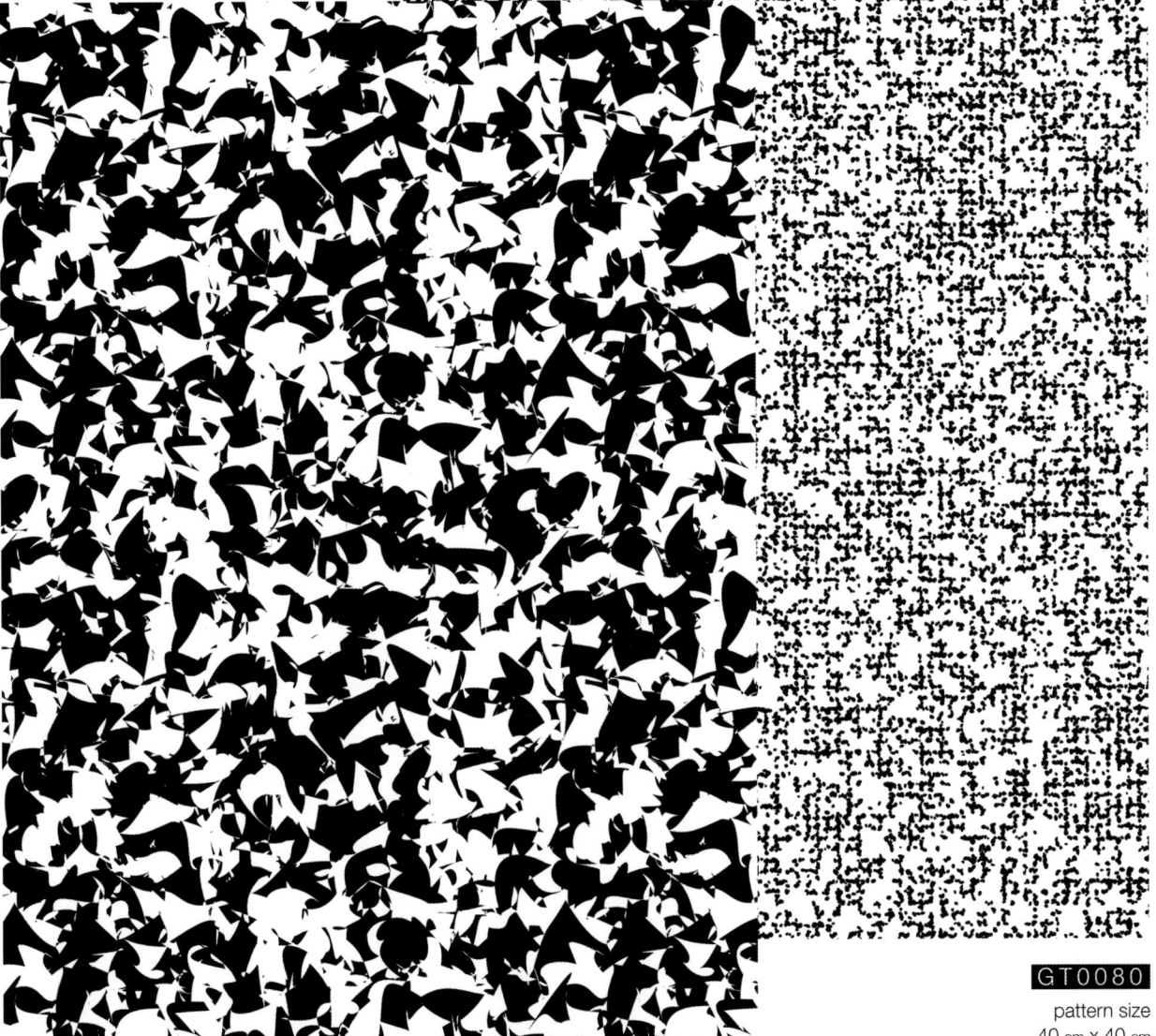

GT0080
pattern size
40 cm x 40 cm

GT0081

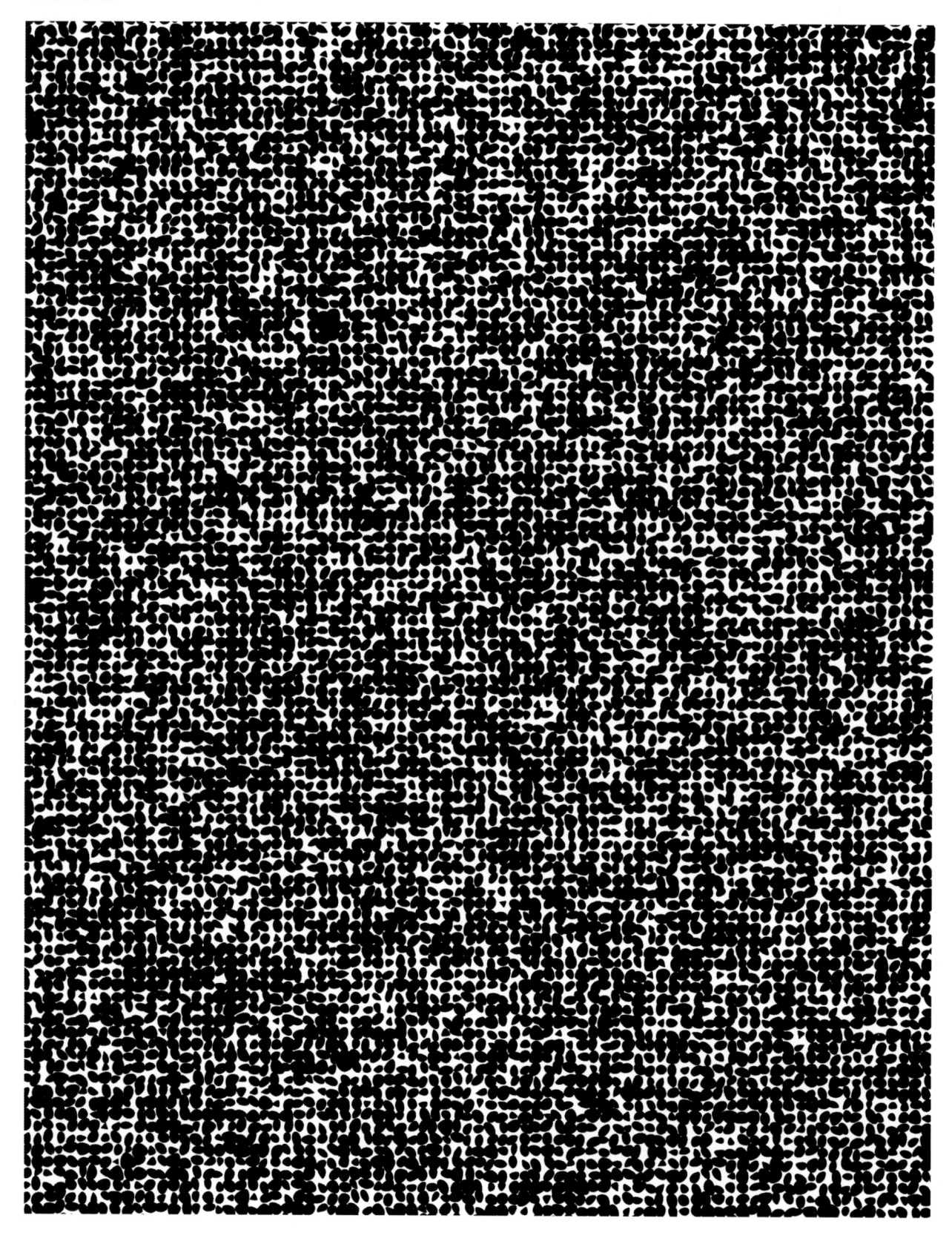

pattern size
40 cm x 40 cm

GT0082

pattern size
40 cm x 40 cm

071

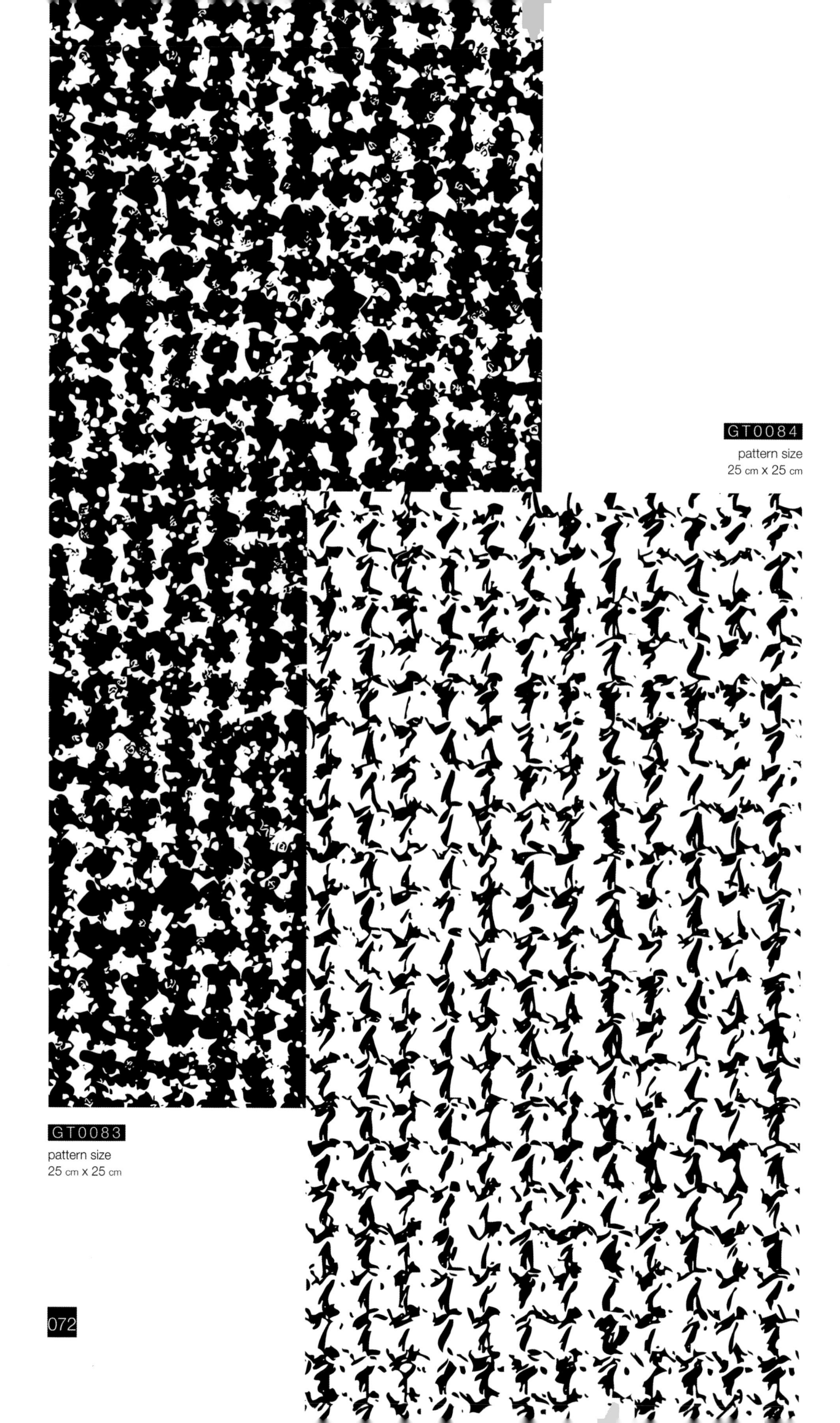

GT0084
pattern size
25 cm x 25 cm

GT0083
pattern size
25 cm x 25 cm

072

GT0085

pattern size
40 cm x 40 cm

073

GT0086
pattern size
16 cm x 16 cm

074

GT0087

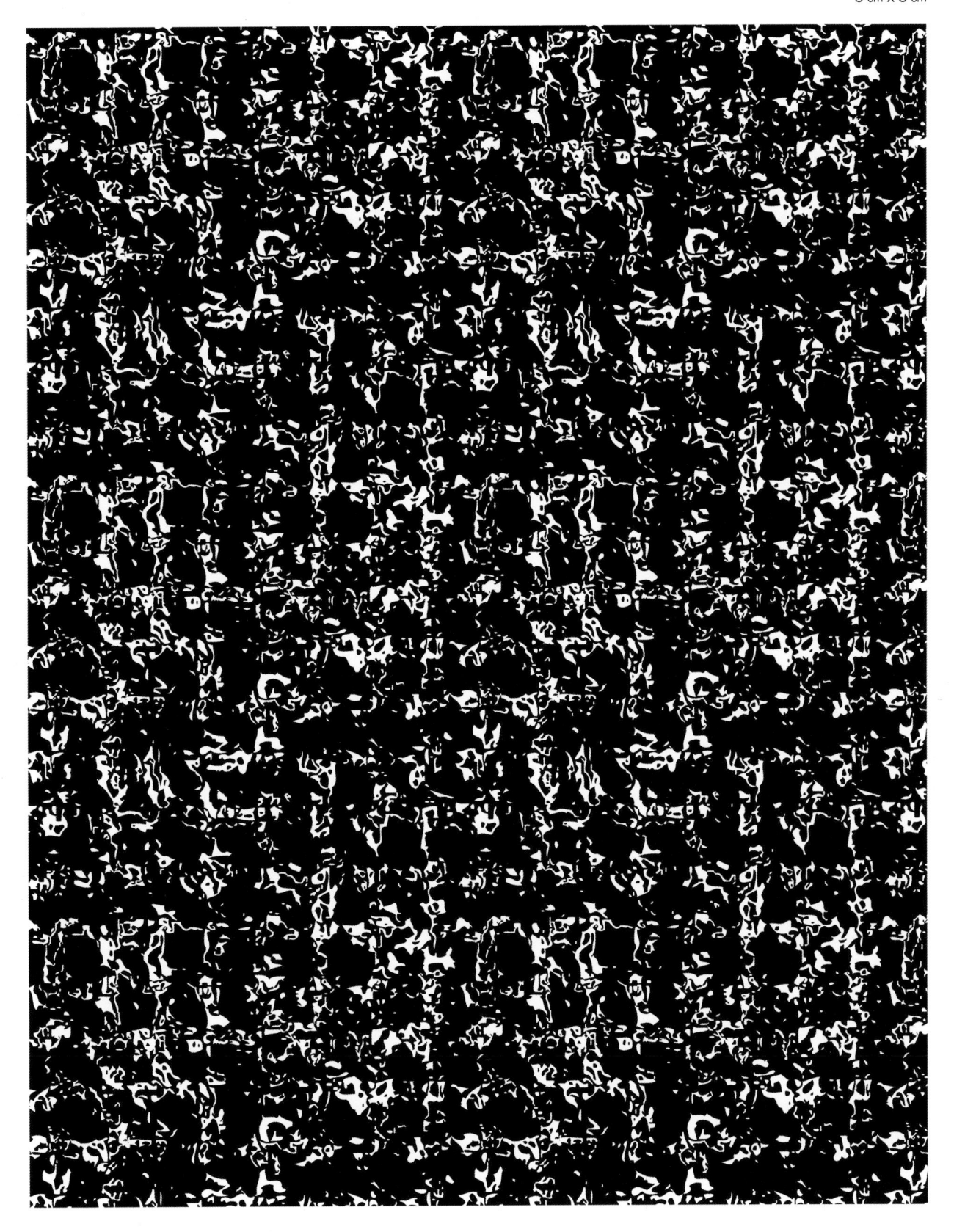

pattern size
8 cm x 8 cm

GT0088

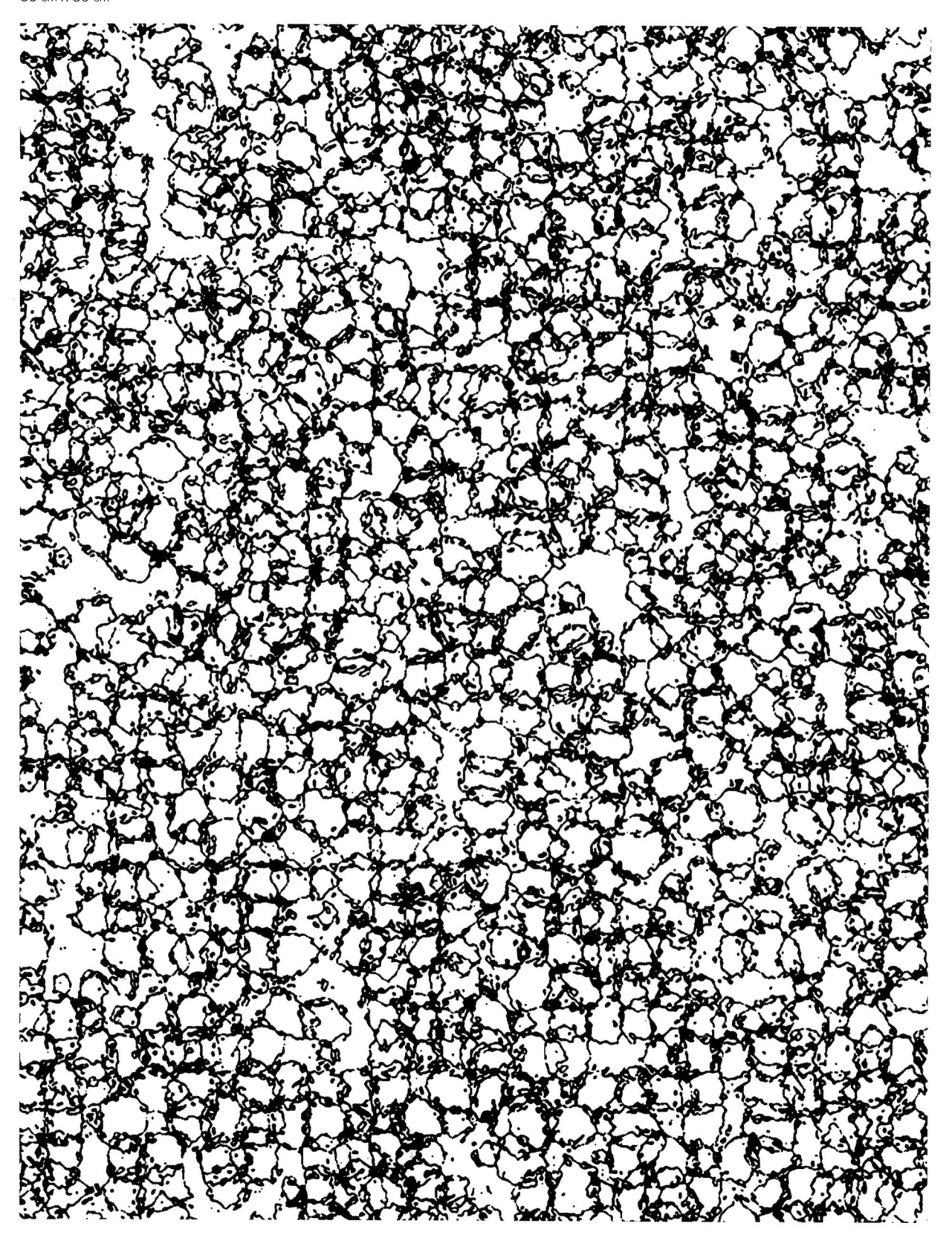

pattern size
30 cm x 30 cm

GT0089

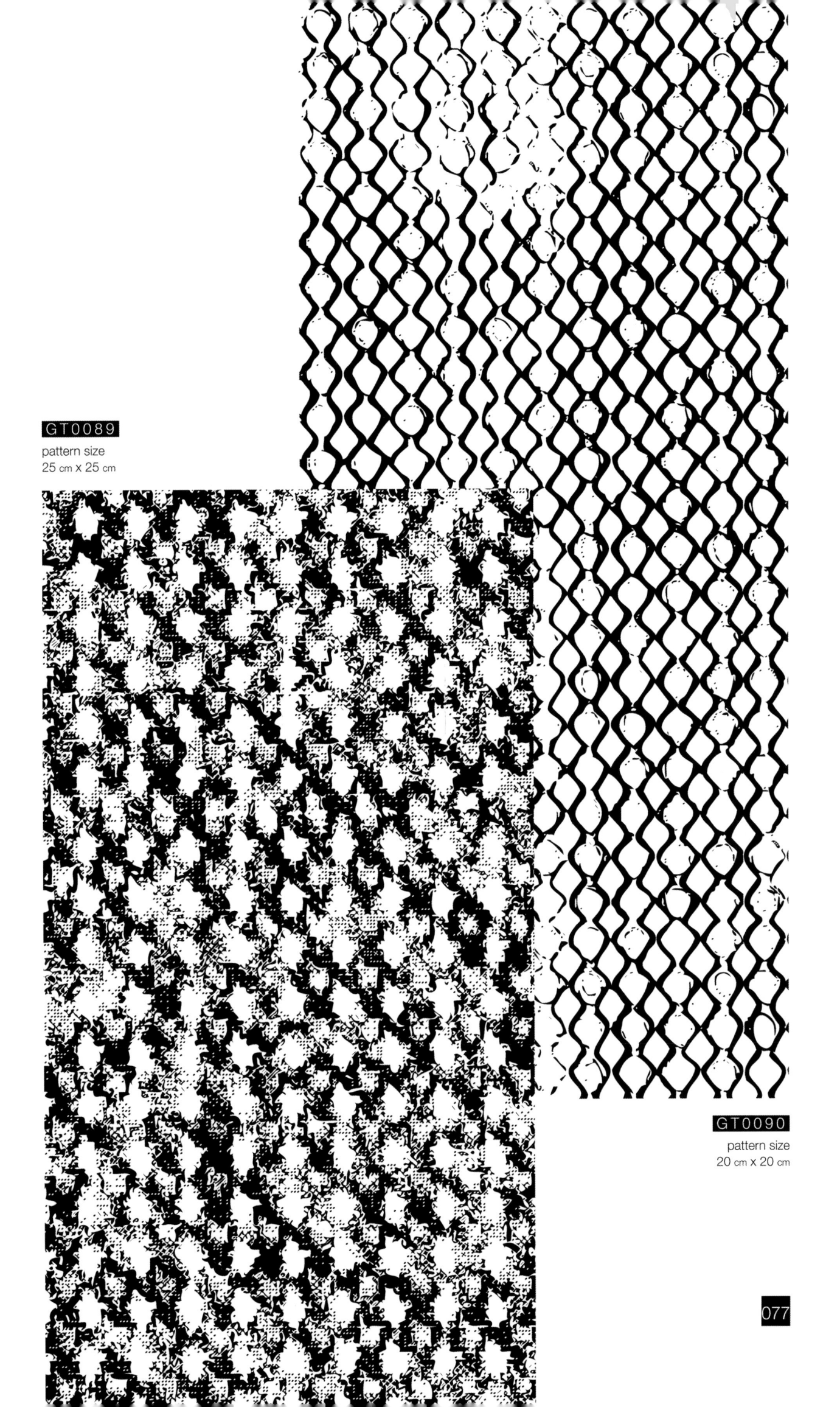

pattern size
25 cm x 25 cm

GT0090

pattern size
20 cm x 20 cm

077

GT0091
pattern size
20 cm x 20 cm

GT0092

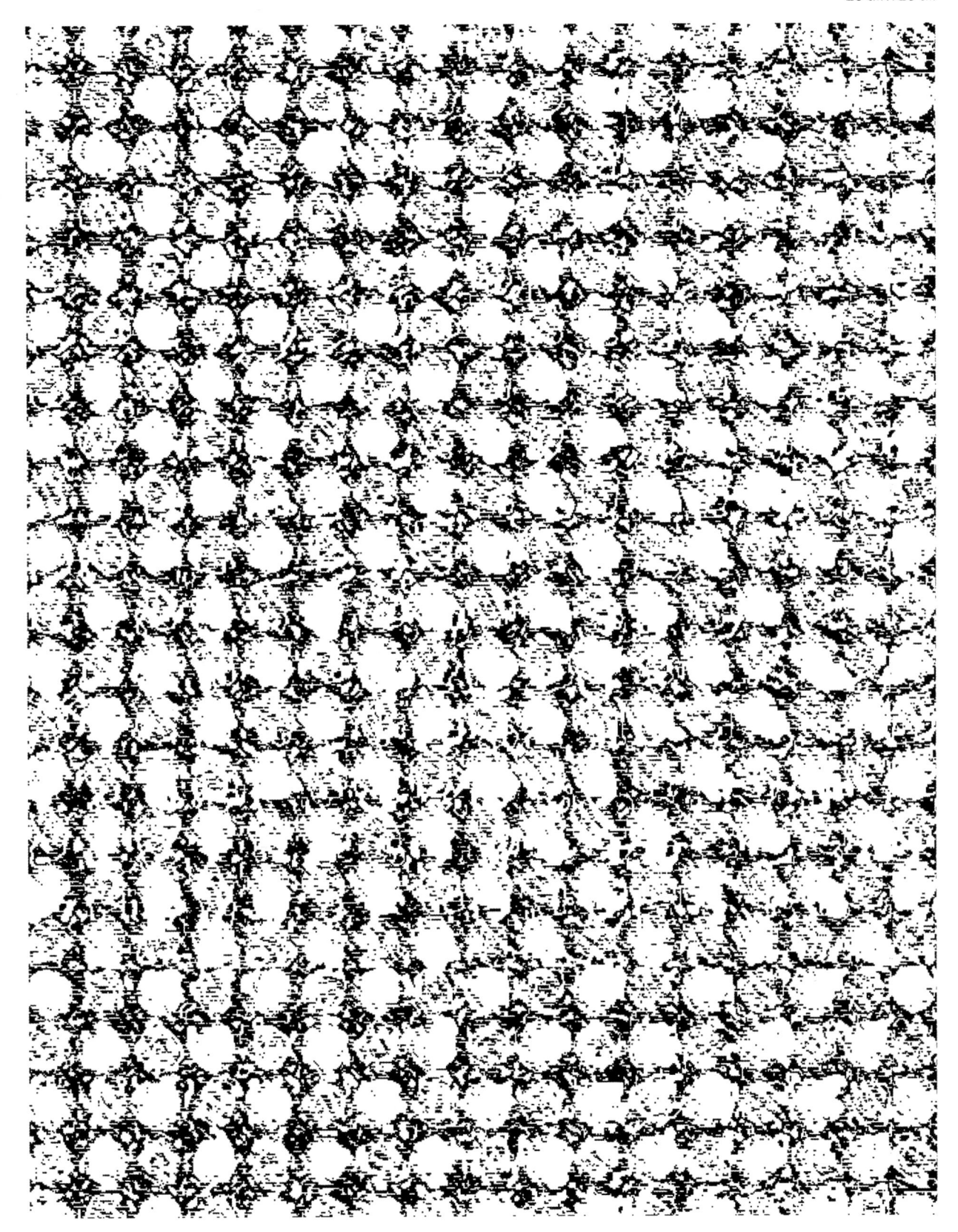

pattern size
20 cm x 20 cm

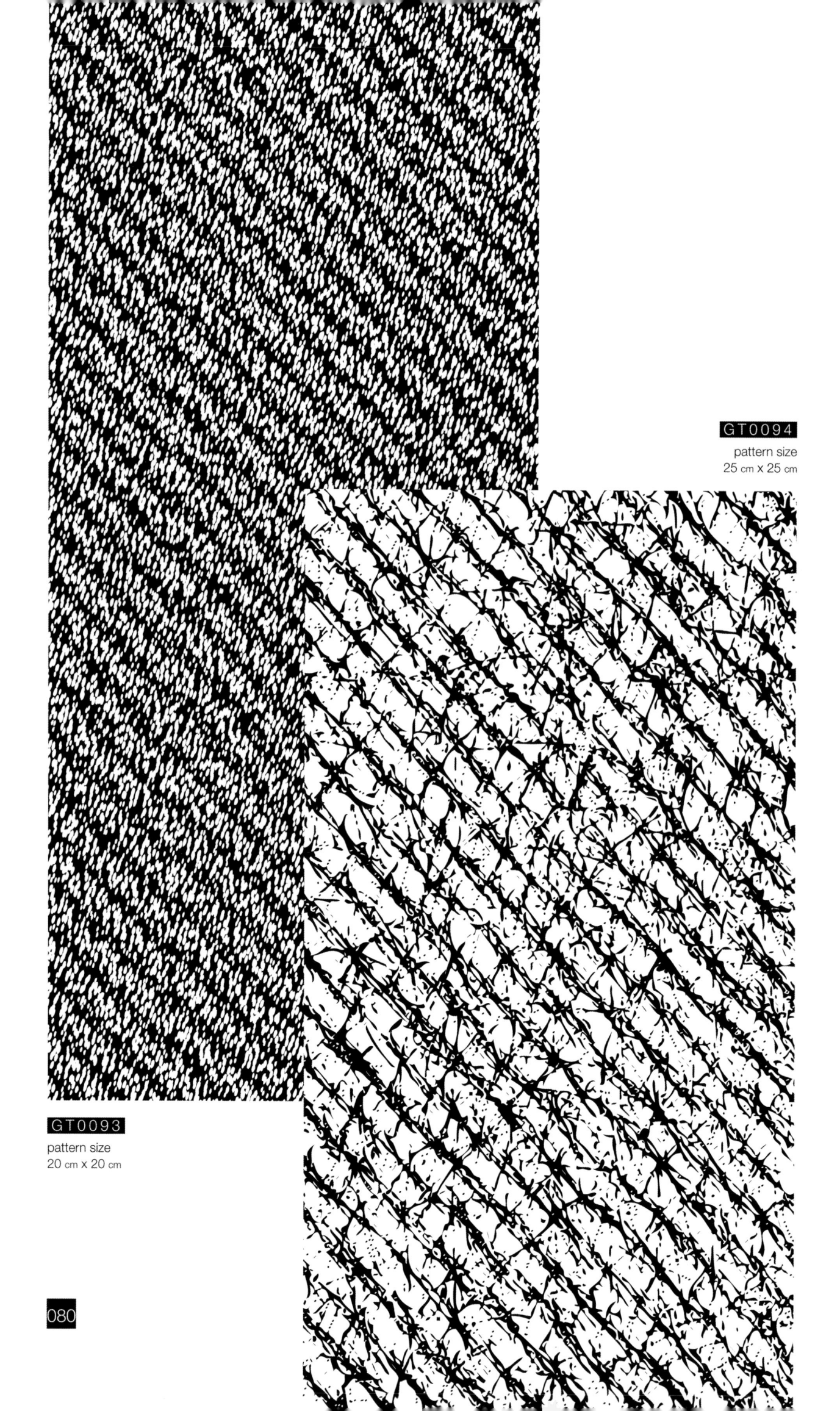

GT0094
pattern size
25 cm x 25 cm

GT0093
pattern size
20 cm x 20 cm

GT0095

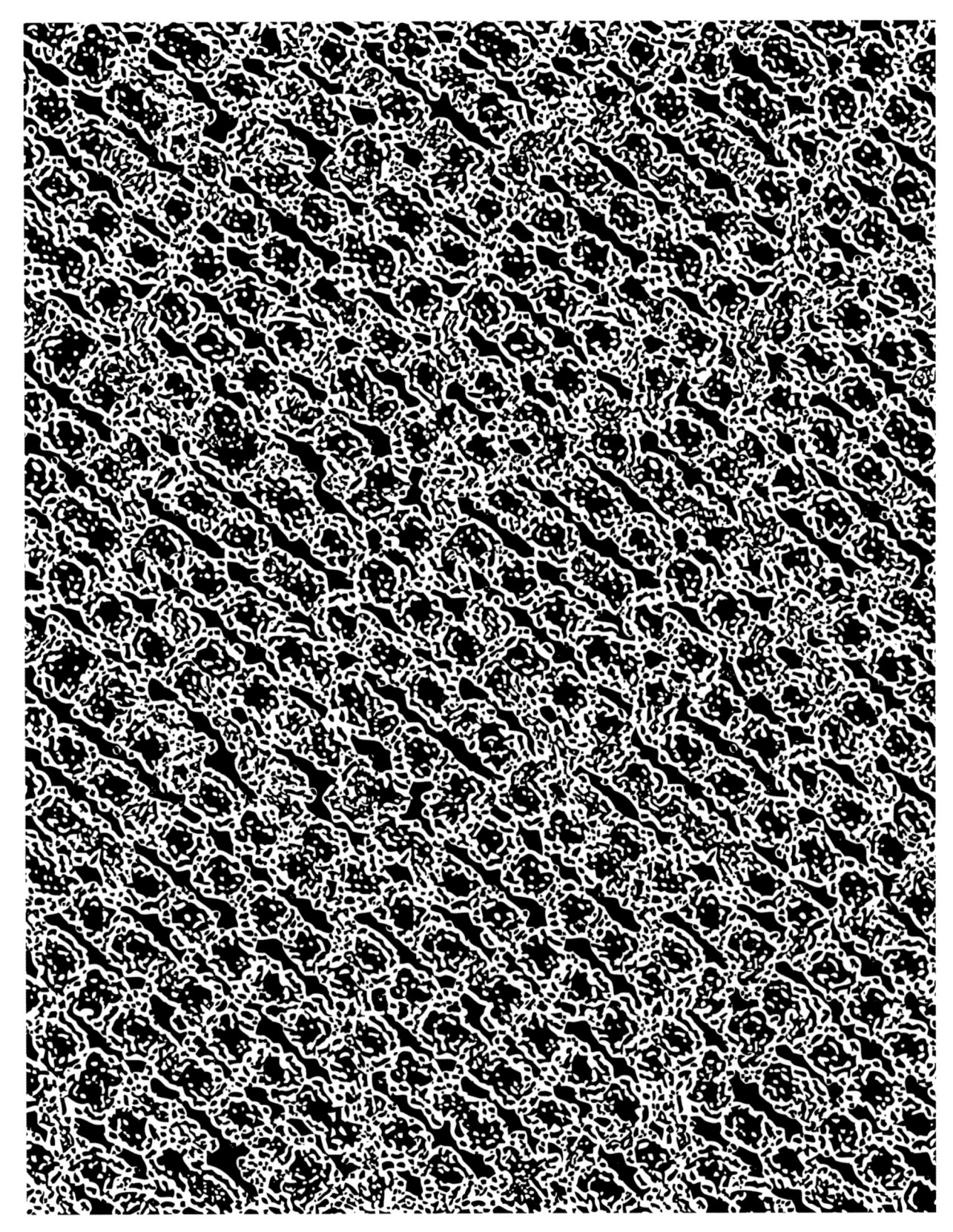

pattern size
20 cm x 20 cm

## GT0096

pattern size
15 cm x 19 cm

GT0097

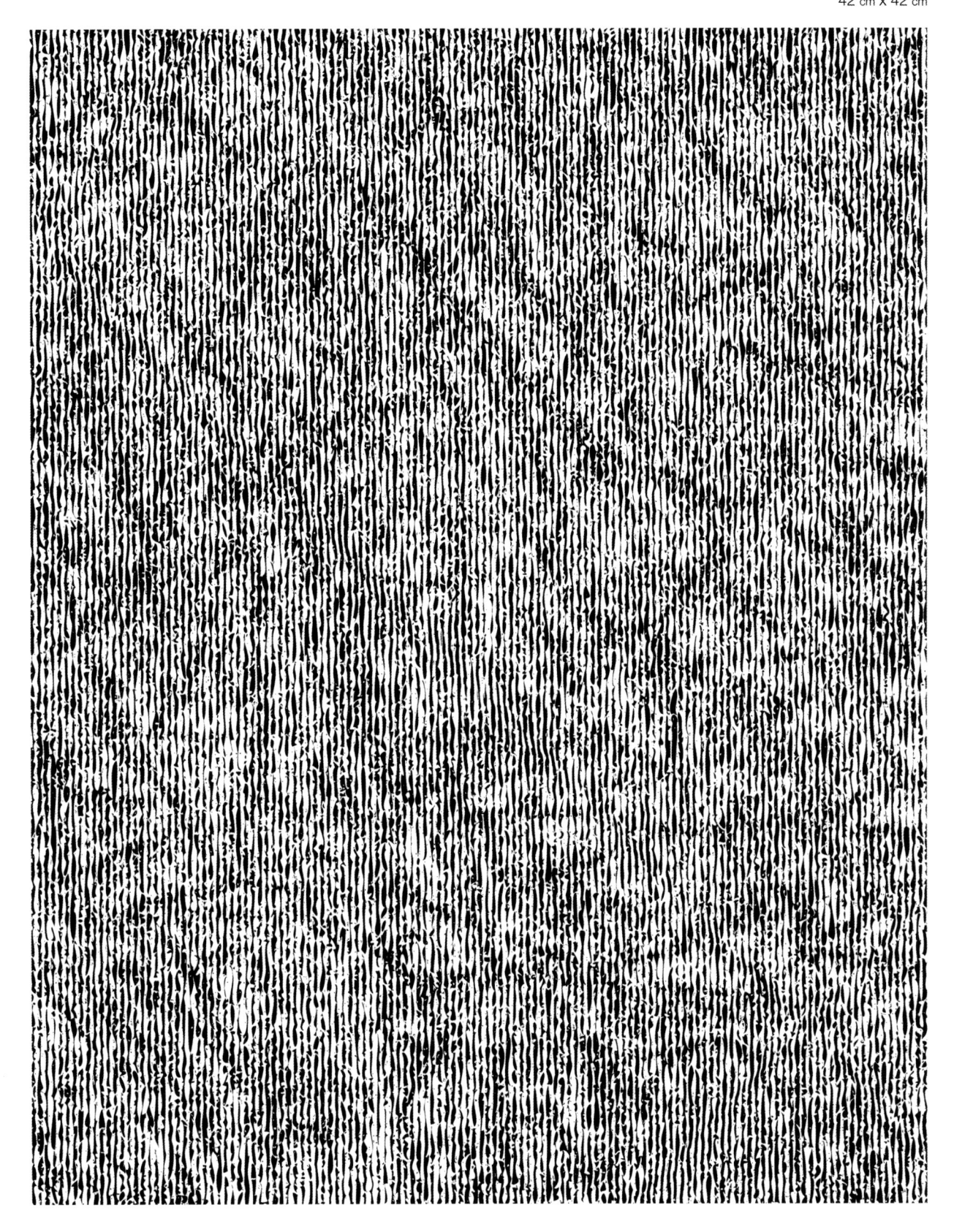

pattern size
42 cm x 42 cm

GT0098
pattern size
41,5 cm x 41,5 cm

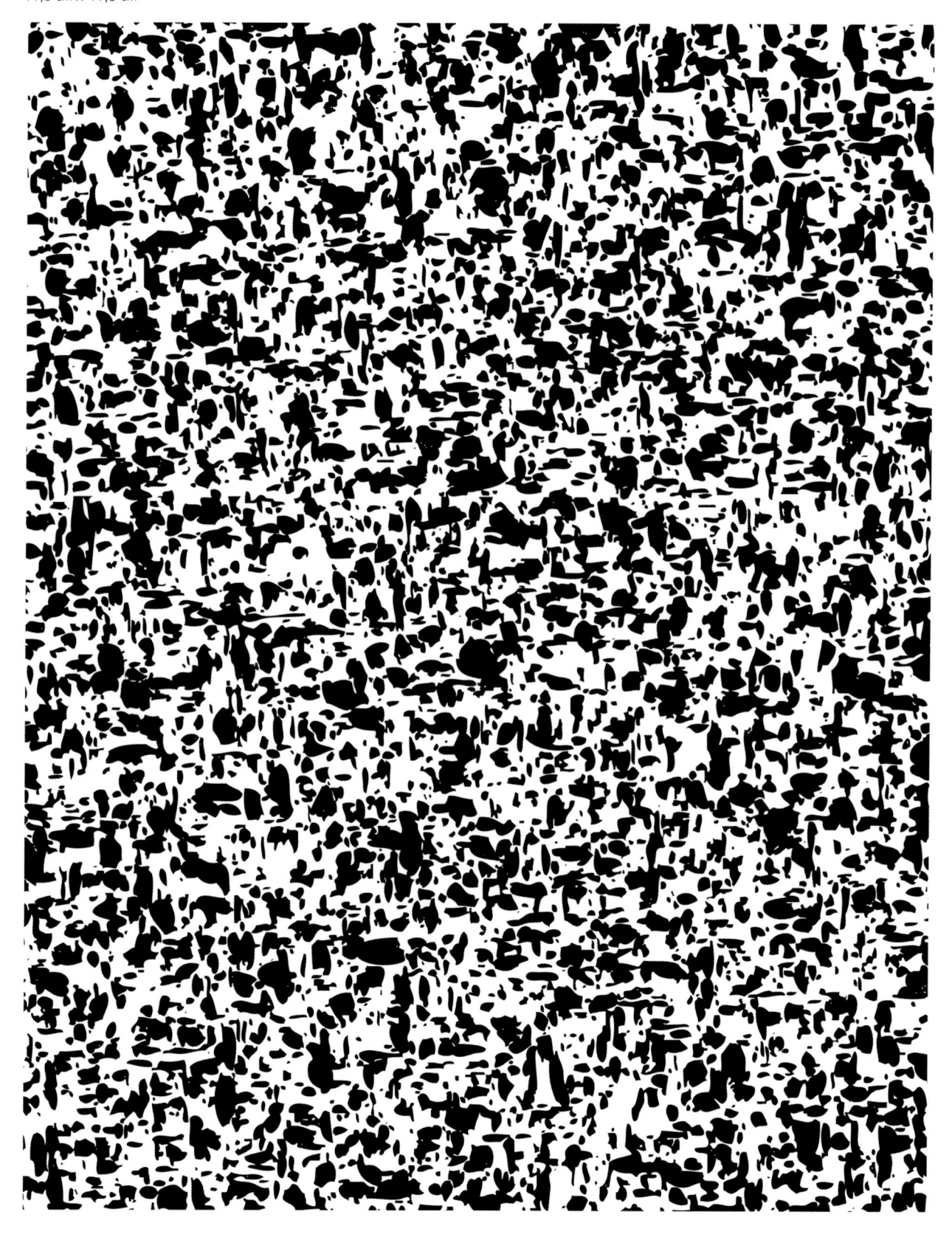

084

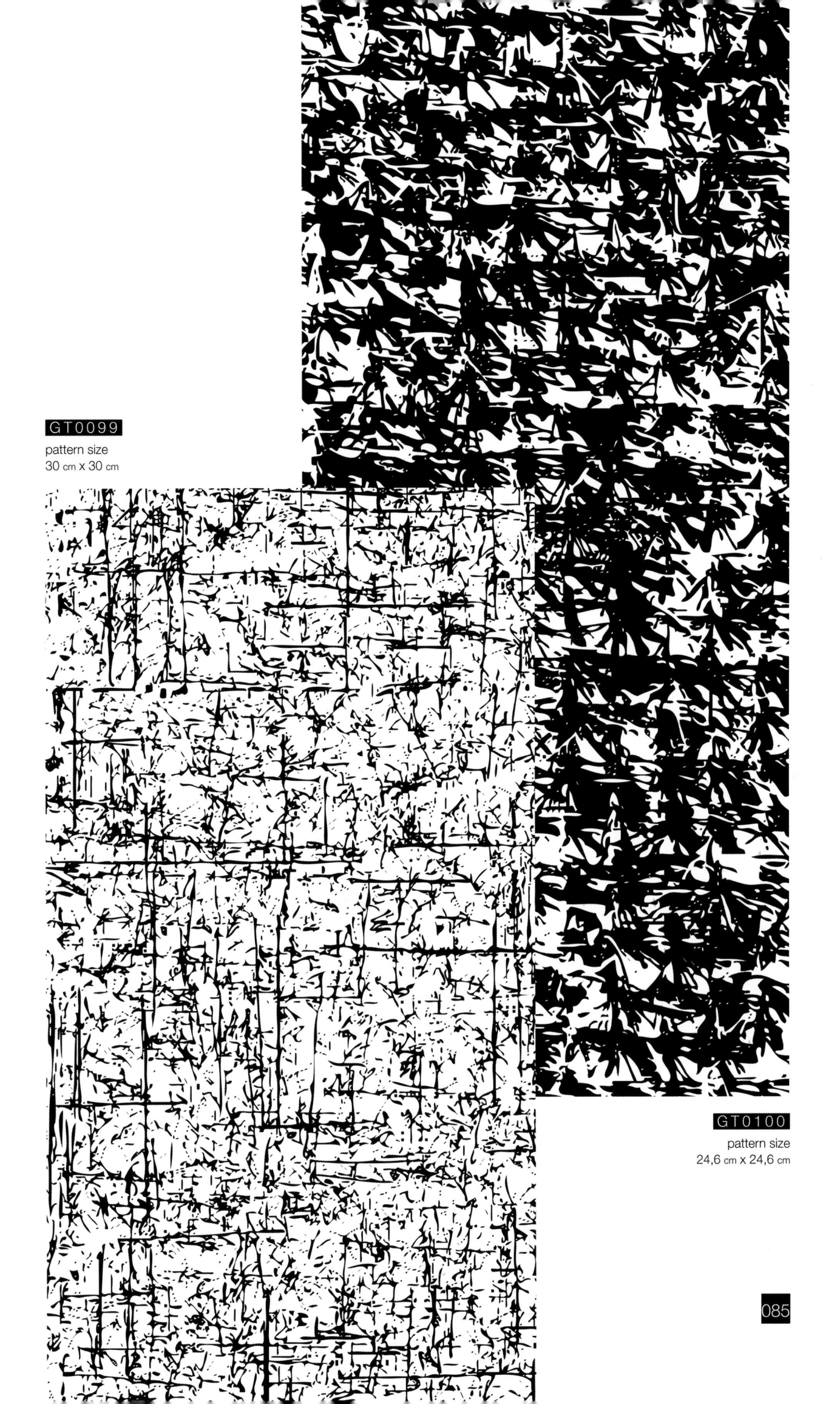

GT0099
pattern size
30 cm x 30 cm

GT0100
pattern size
24,6 cm x 24,6 cm

085

GT0101

pattern size
33,3 cm x 33,3 cm

GT0102

pattern size
24 cm x 24 cm

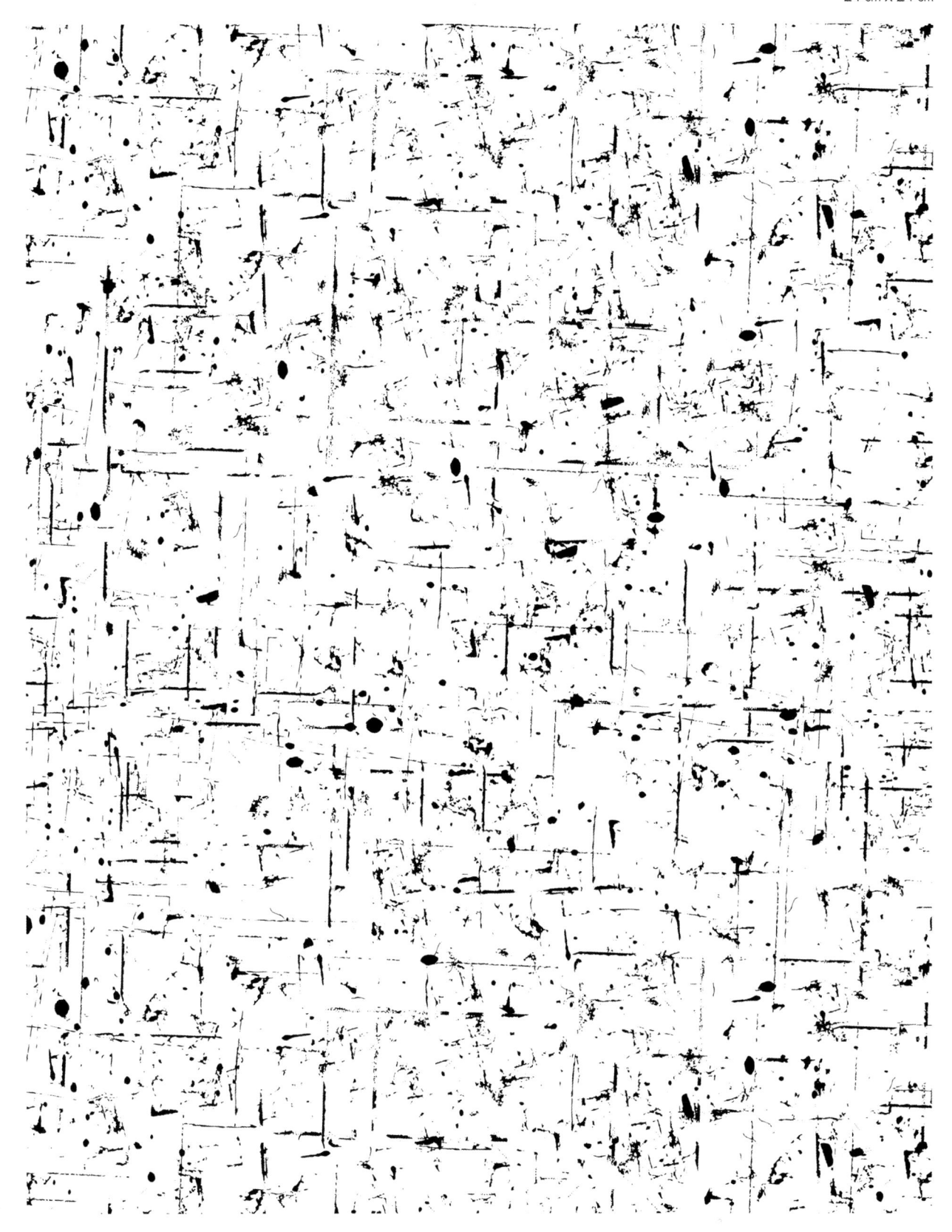

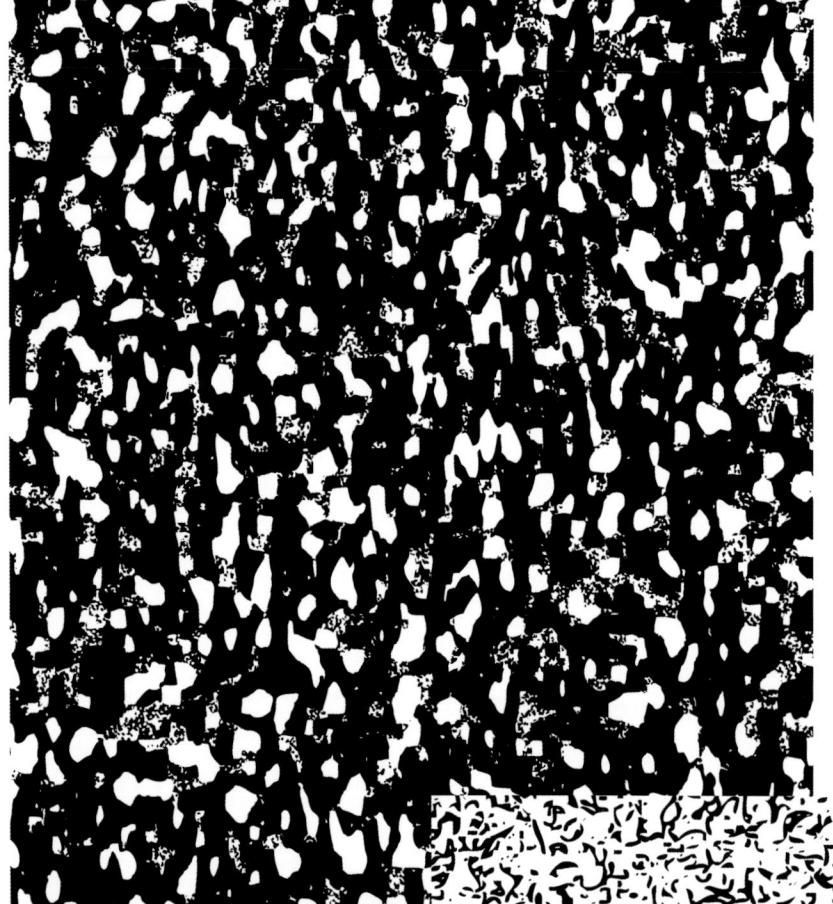

GT0104
pattern size
20 cm x 20 cm

GT0103
pattern size
20 cm x 20 cm

088

GT0105

pattern size
20 cm x 20 cm

GT0106
pattern size
16,5 cm x 16,5 cm

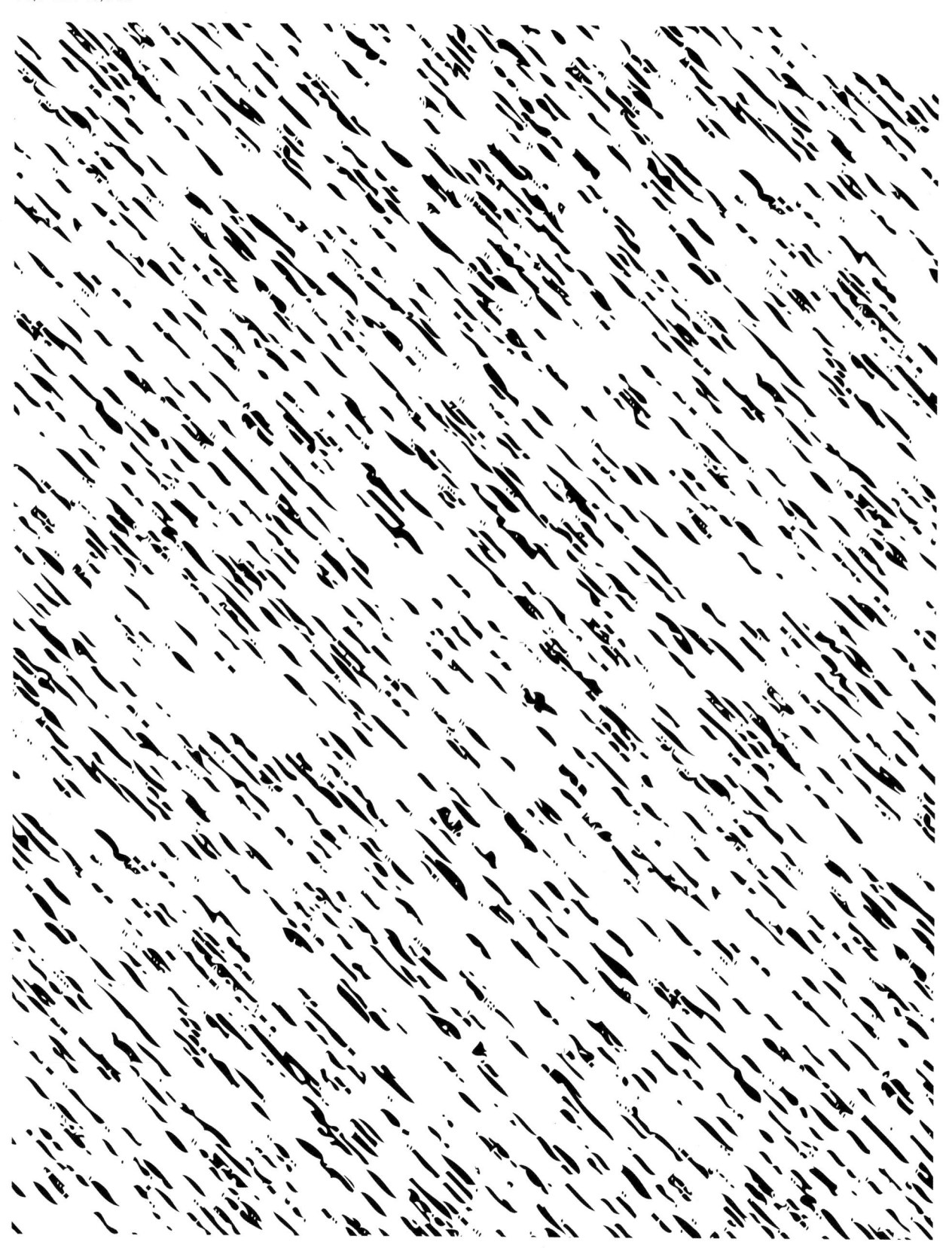

GT0107
pattern size
20 cm x 20 cm

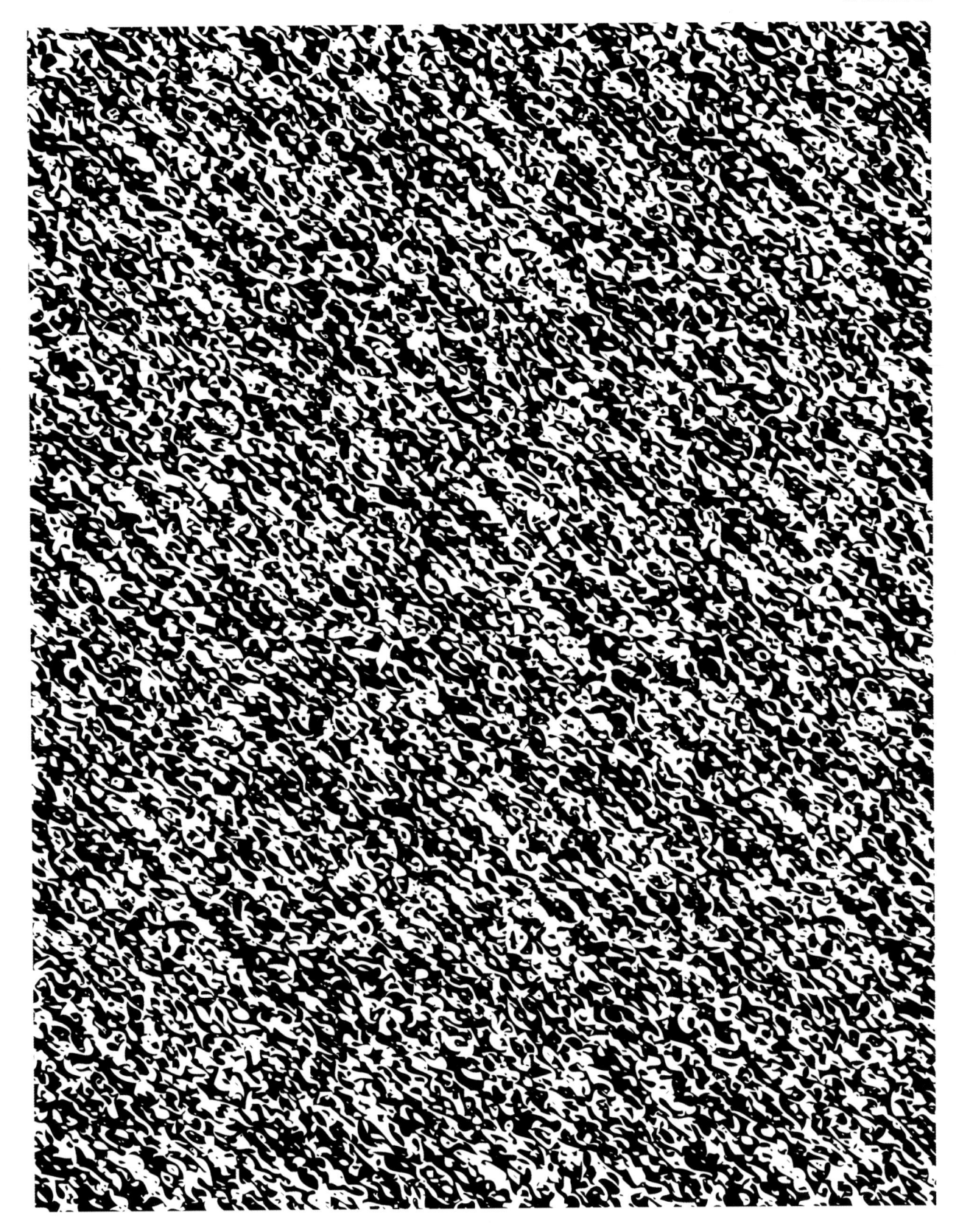

GT0108
pattern size
12 cm x 12 cm

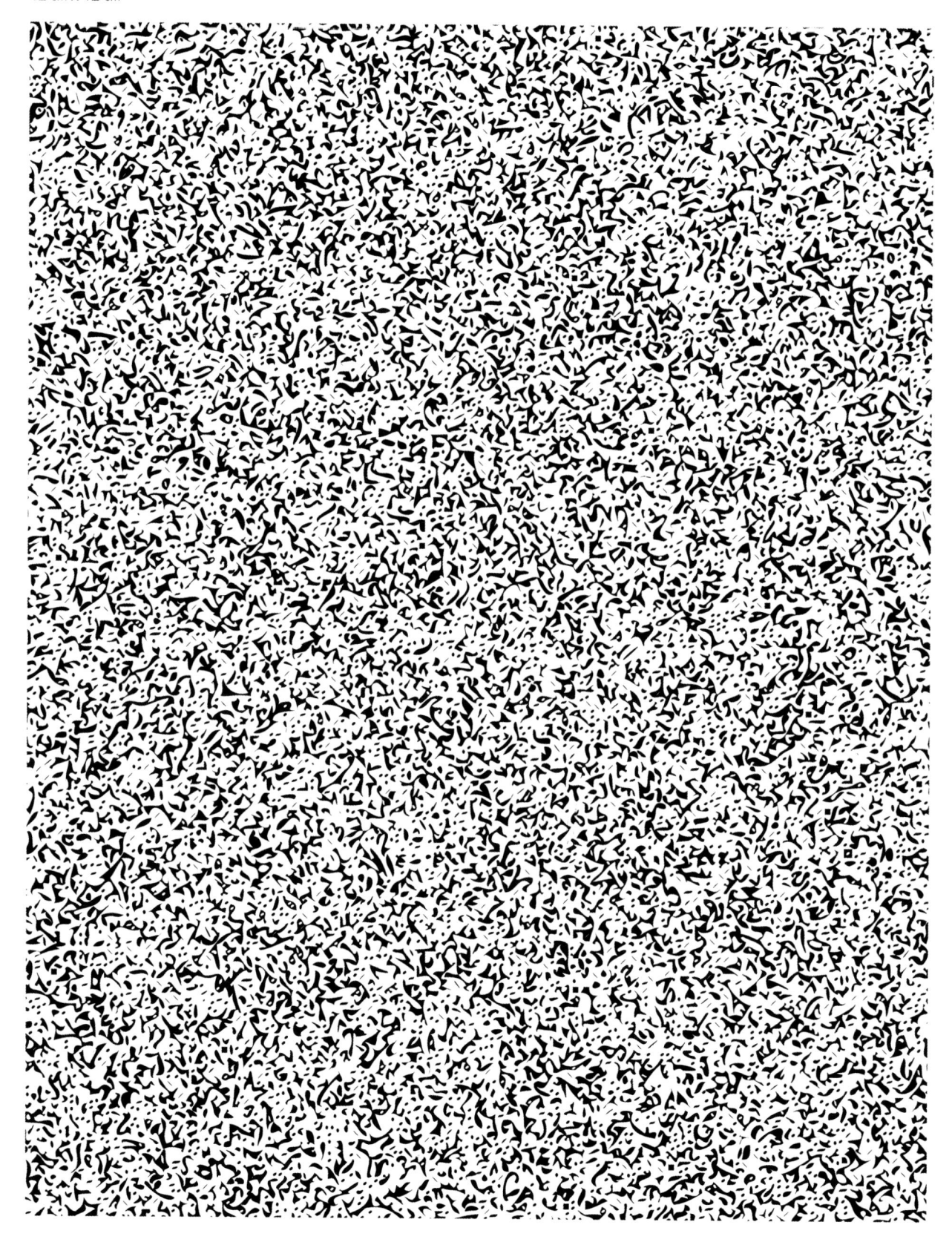

GT0109
pattern size
12 cm x 12 cm

GT0110
pattern size
20 cm x 20 cm

093

GT0111

pattern size
35 cm x 21 cm

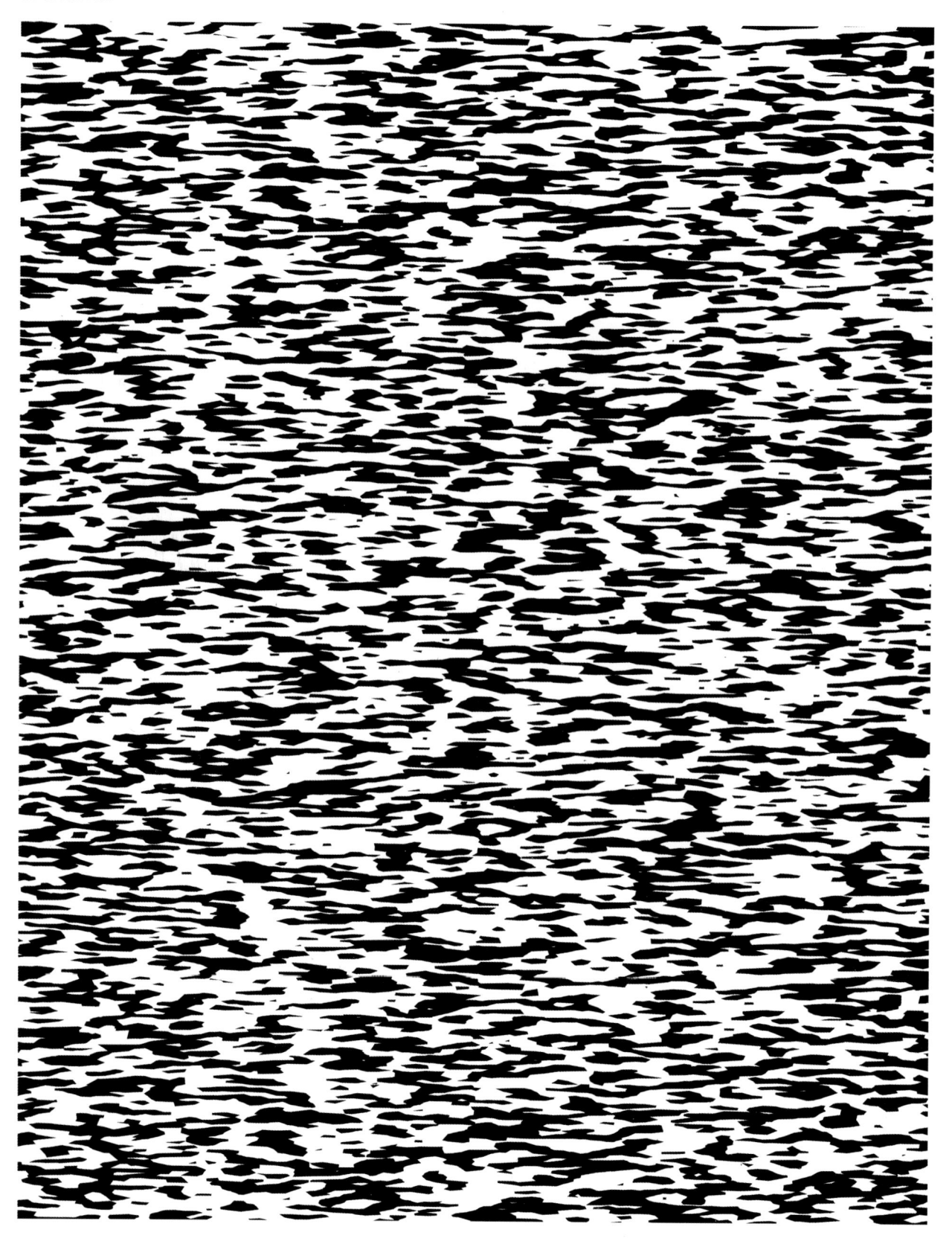

GT0112

pattern size
24 cm x 36 cm

GT0114
pattern size
10 cm x 10 cm

GT0113
pattern size
20 cm x 15 cm

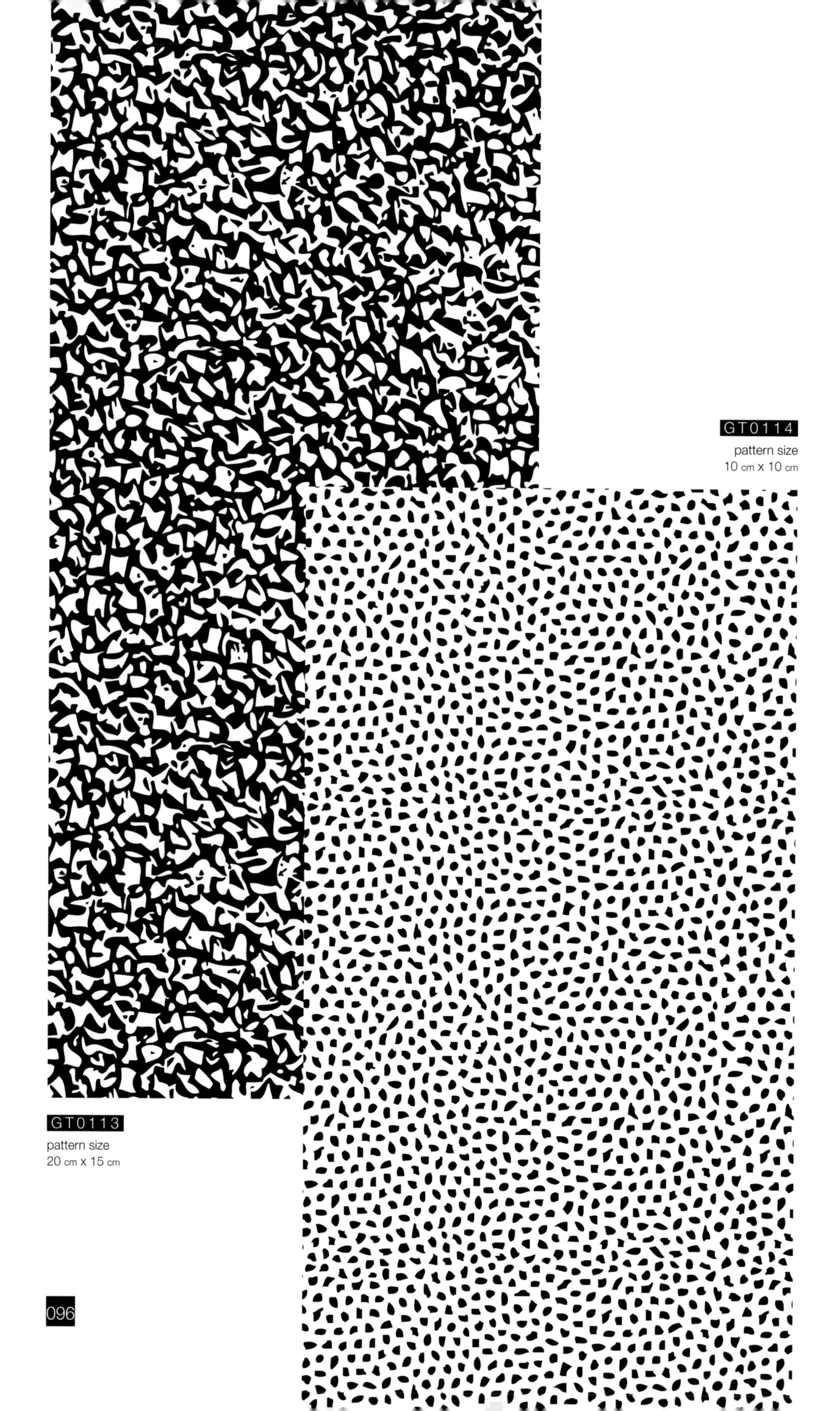

GT0115
pattern size
40 cm x 40 cm

GT0116
pattern size
29,5 cm x 29,5 cm

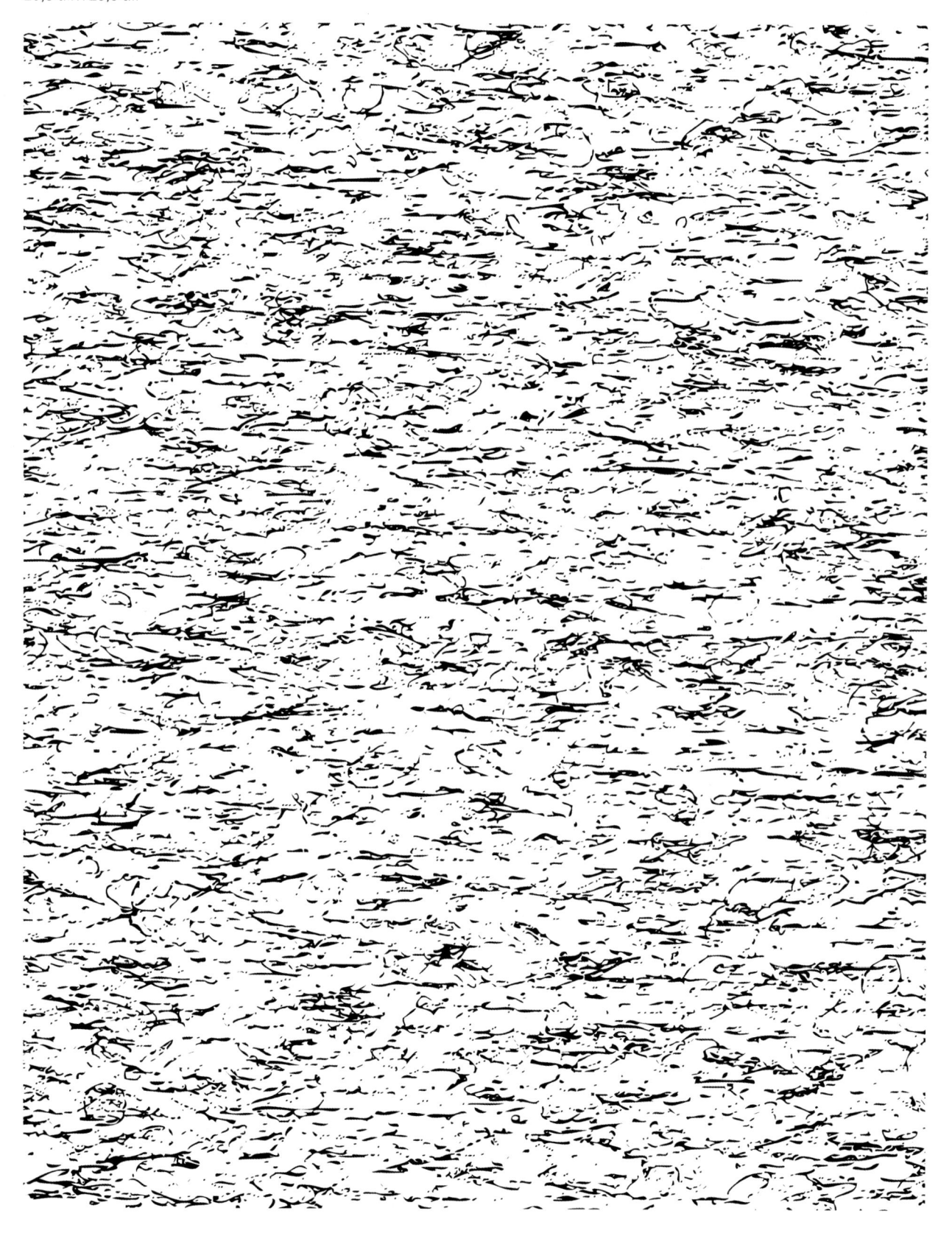

GT0117

pattern size
21 cm x 21 cm

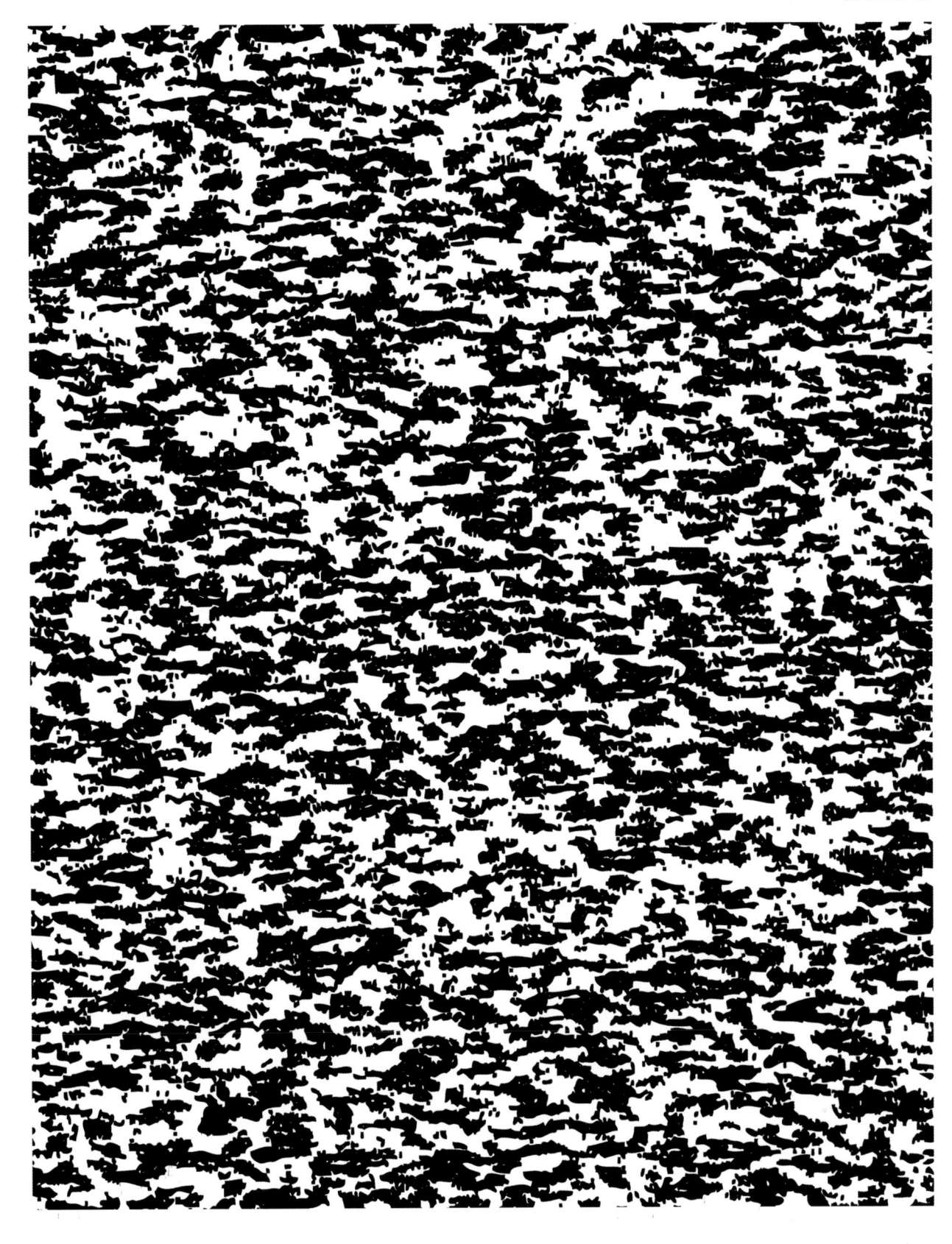

GT0118

pattern size
20 cm x 20 cm

GT0119
pattern size
37,5 cm x 37,5 cm

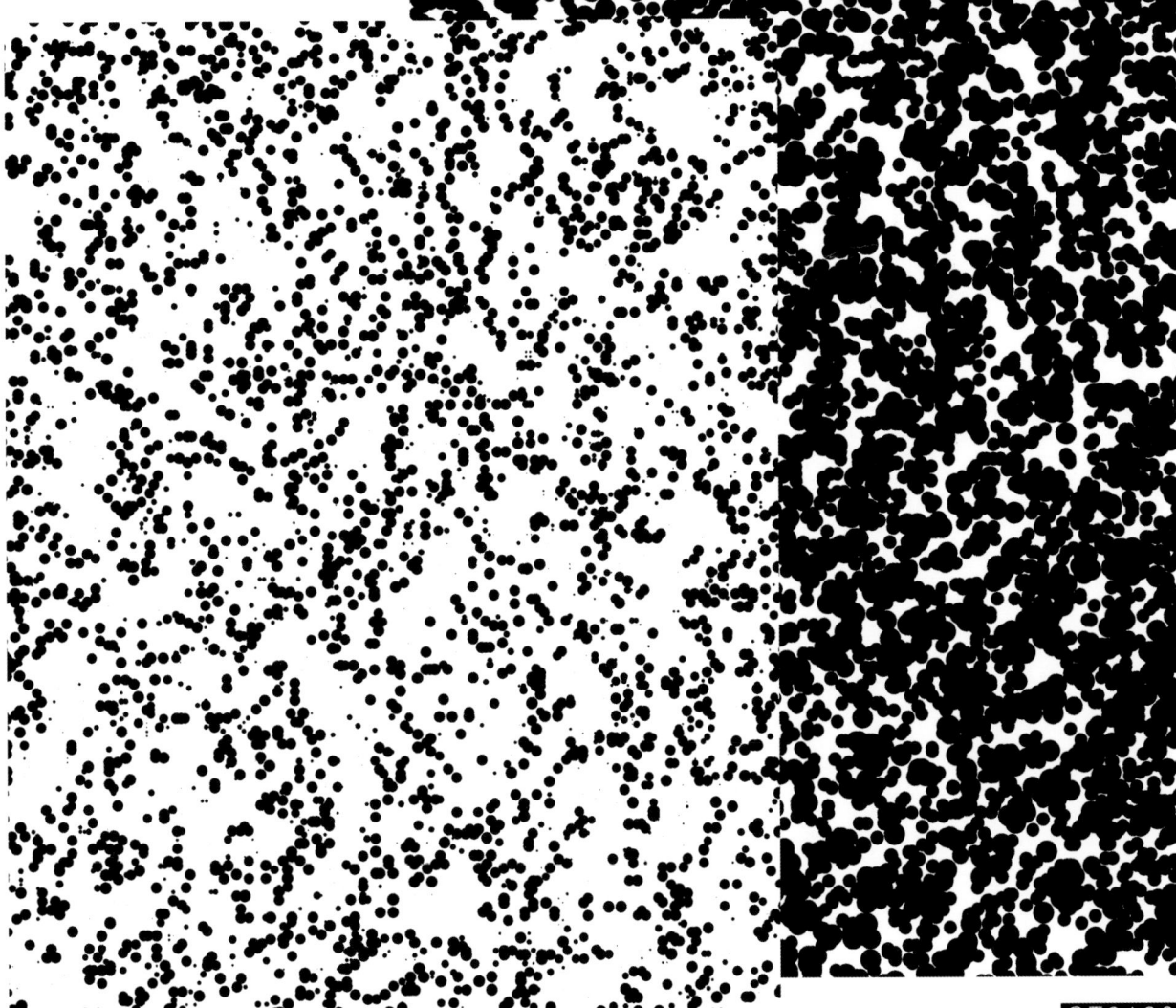

GT0120
pattern size
29 cm x 29 cm

101

GT0121

pattern size
30 cm x 30 cm

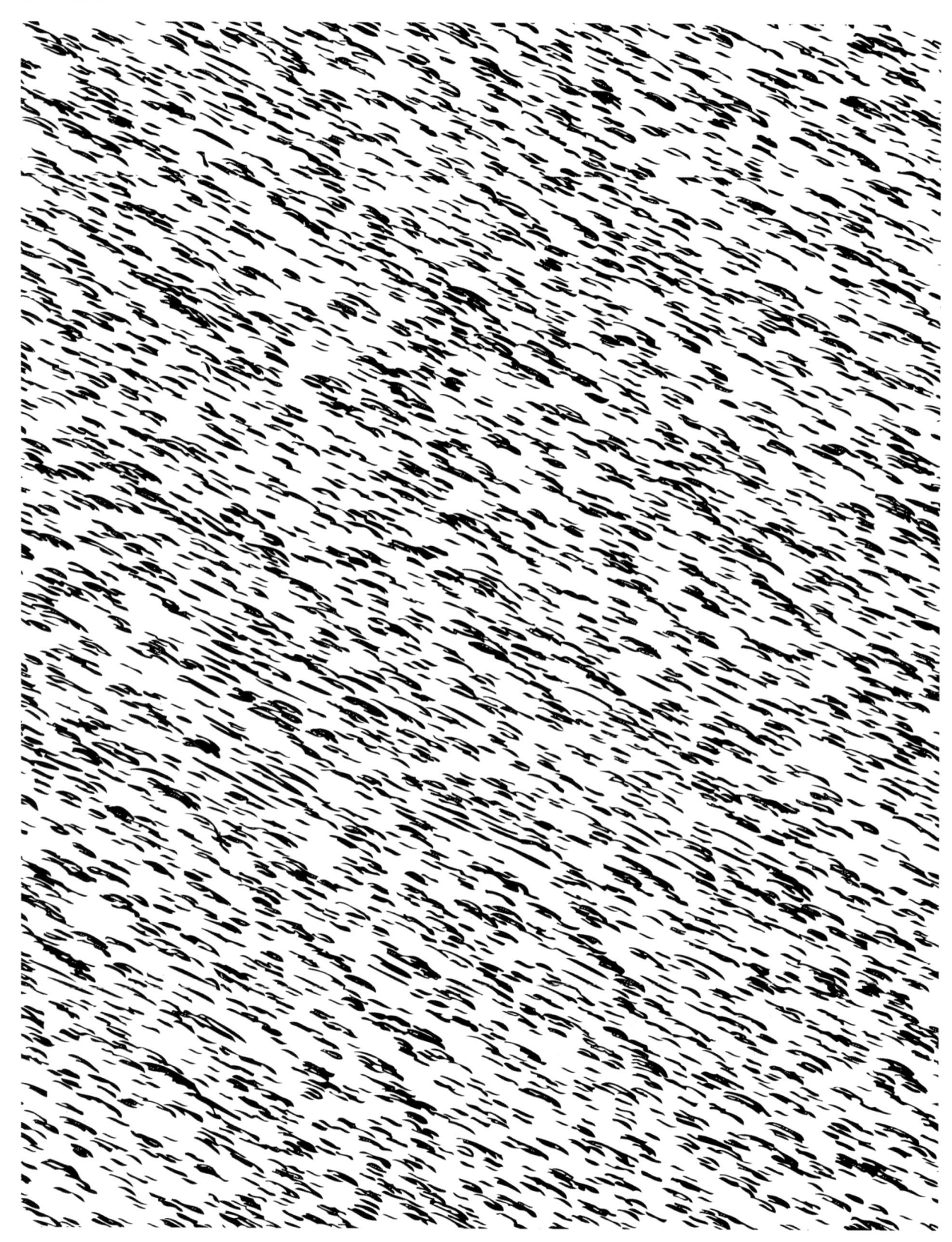

GT0122

pattern size
25 cm x 25 cm

GT0124
pattern size
42,5 cm x 42,5 cm

GT0123
pattern size
30 cm x 15 cm

GT0125

pattern size
33 cm x 33 cm

GT0126
pattern size
33,5 cm x 17,75 cm

GT0127

pattern size
55,7 cm x 55,7 cm

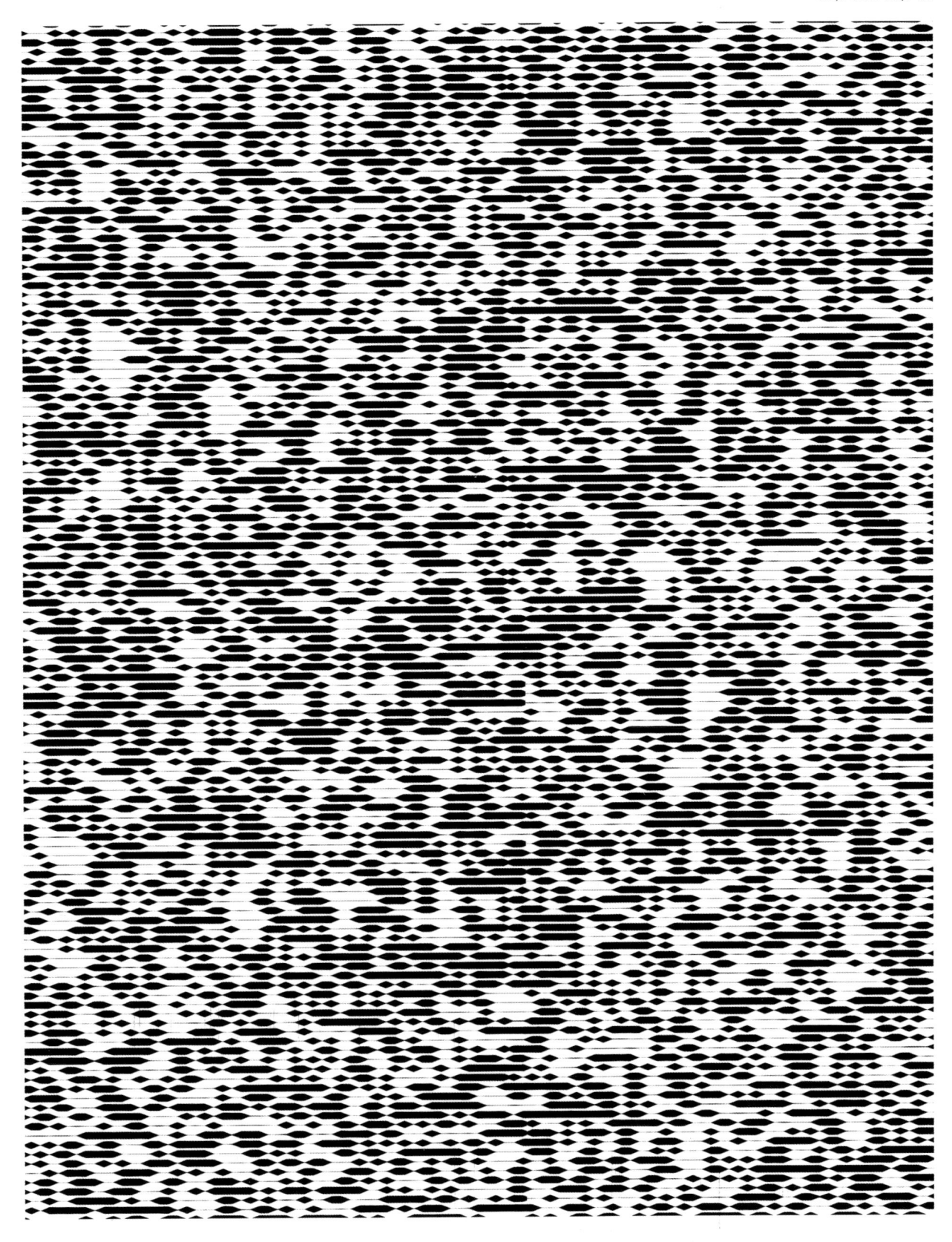

GT0128

pattern size
34,2 cm x 34,2 cm

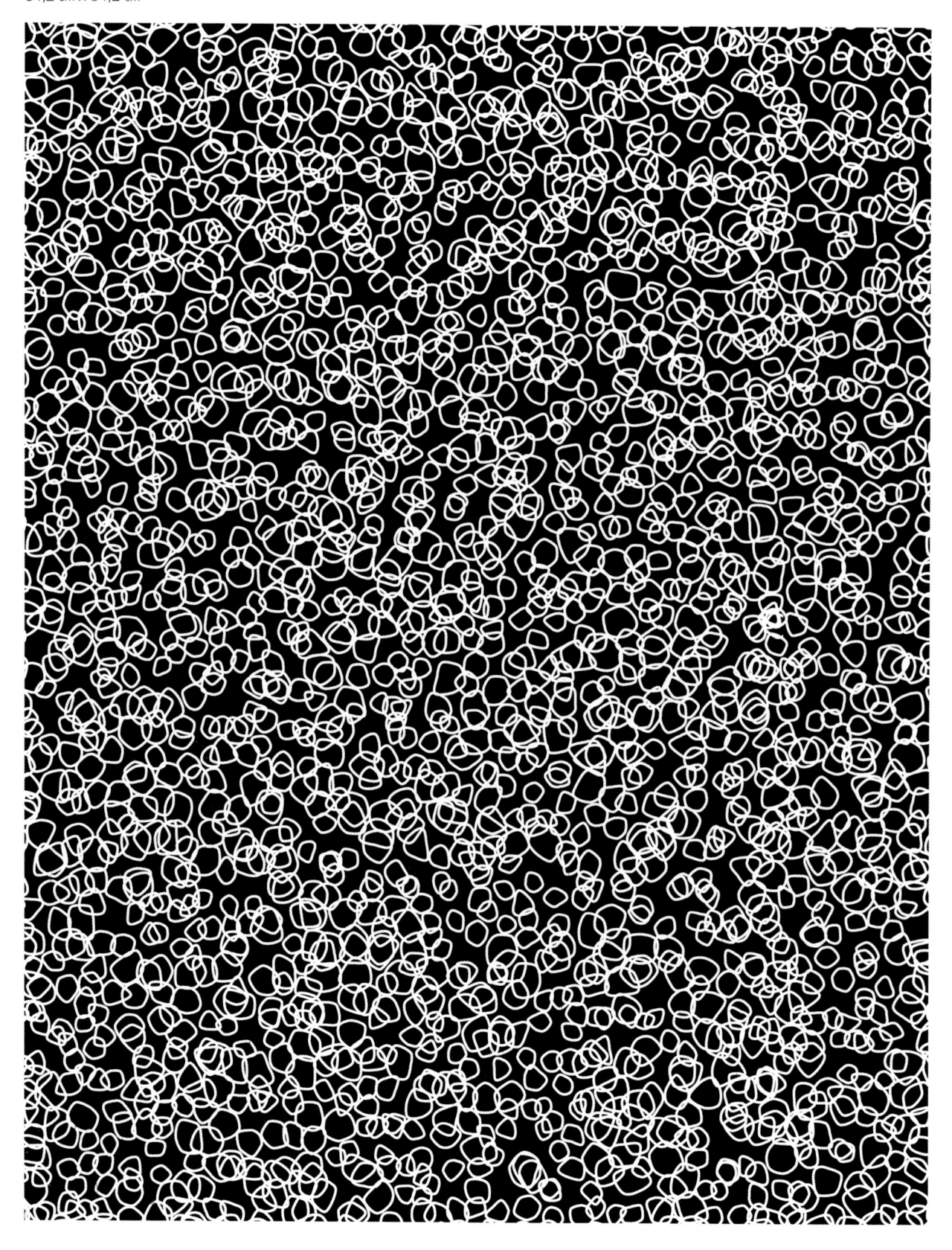

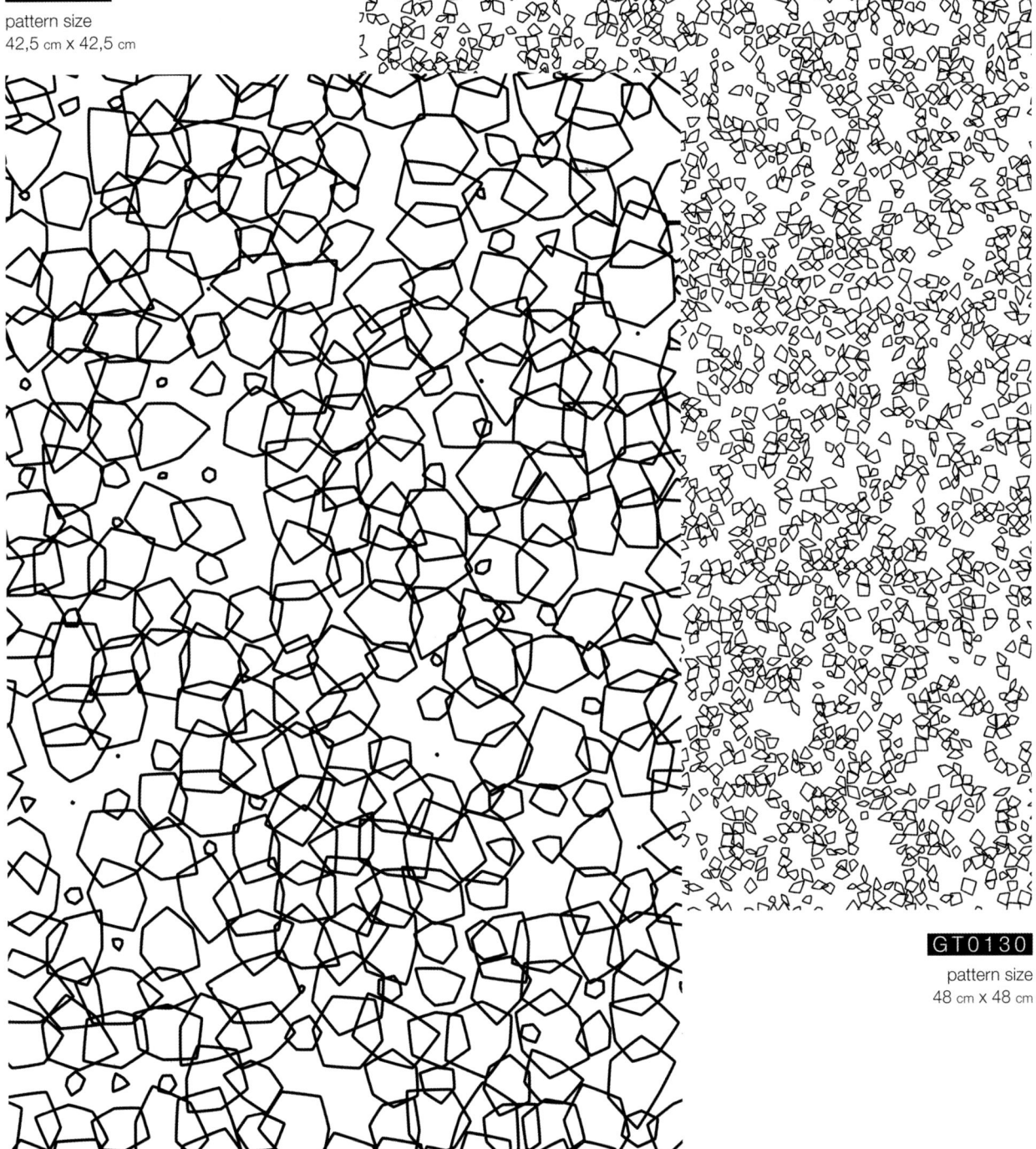

GT0129
pattern size
42,5 cm x 42,5 cm

GT0130
pattern size
48 cm x 48 cm

GT0131

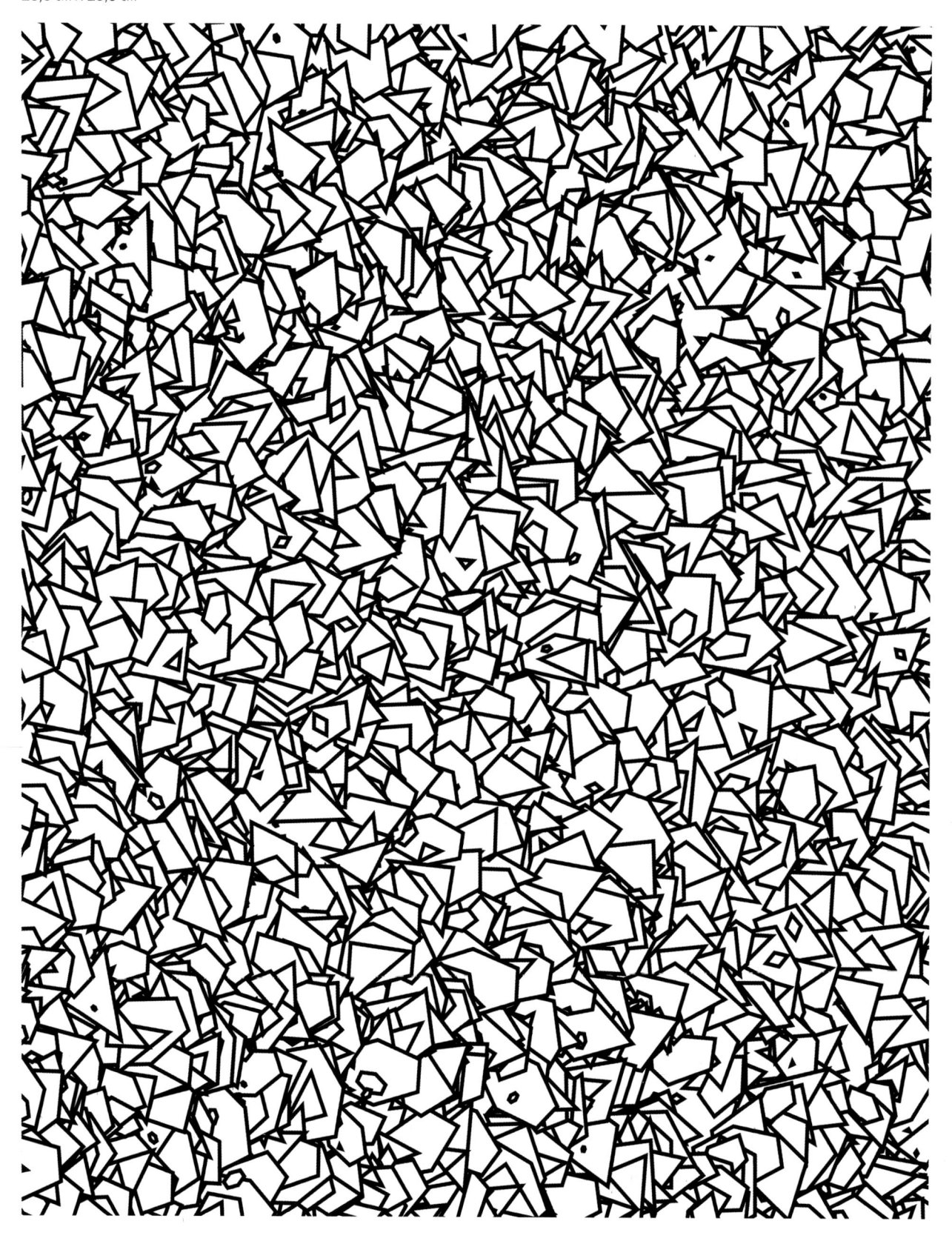

pattern size
28,3 cm x 28,3 cm

GT0132

pattern size
88,5 cm x 88,5 cm

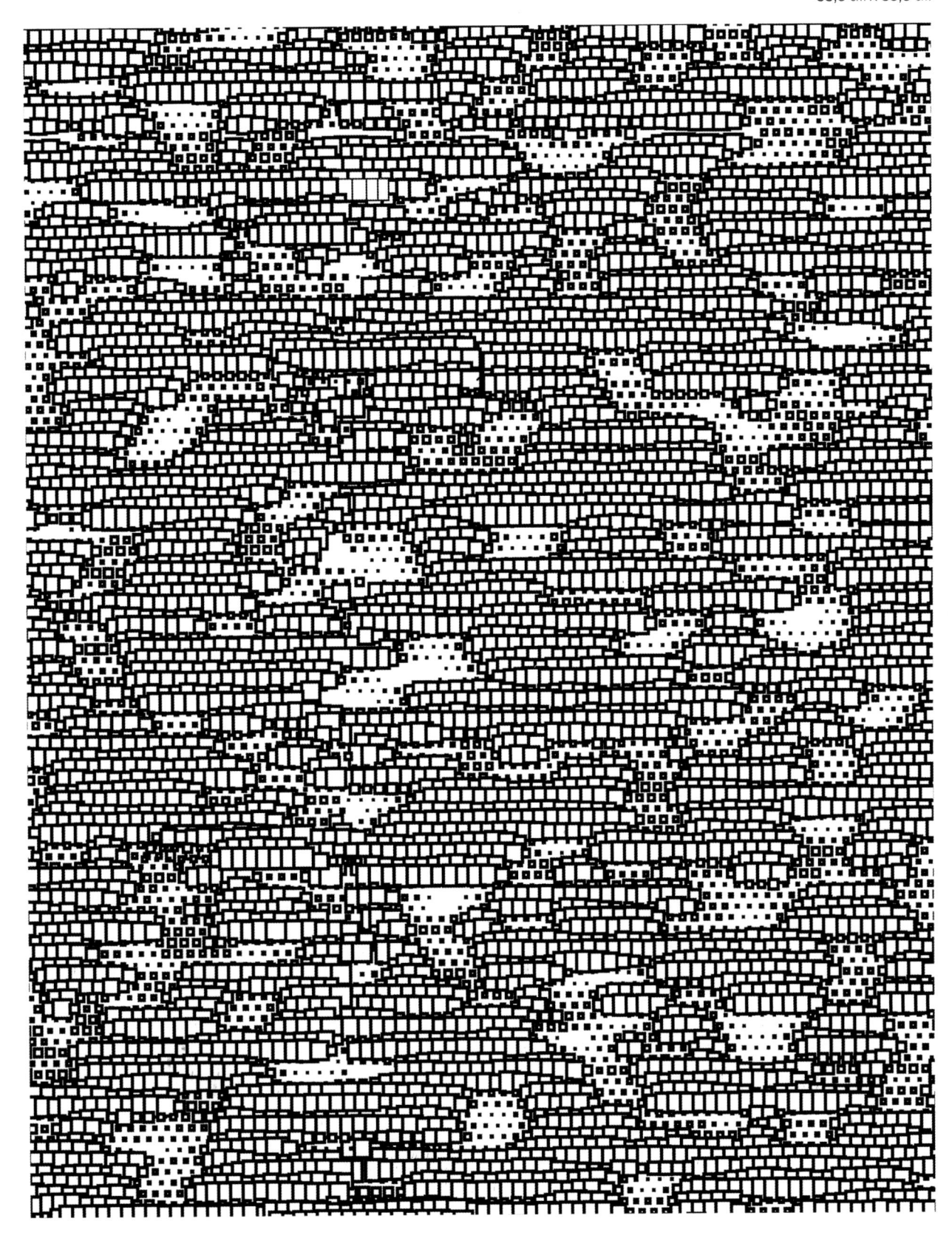

GT0134
pattern size
10 cm x 10 cm

GT0133
pattern size
16cm x 21 cm

GT0135

pattern size
34 cm x 34 cm

## GT0136

pattern size
20 cm x 20 cm

GT0137

pattern size
20 cm x 20 cm

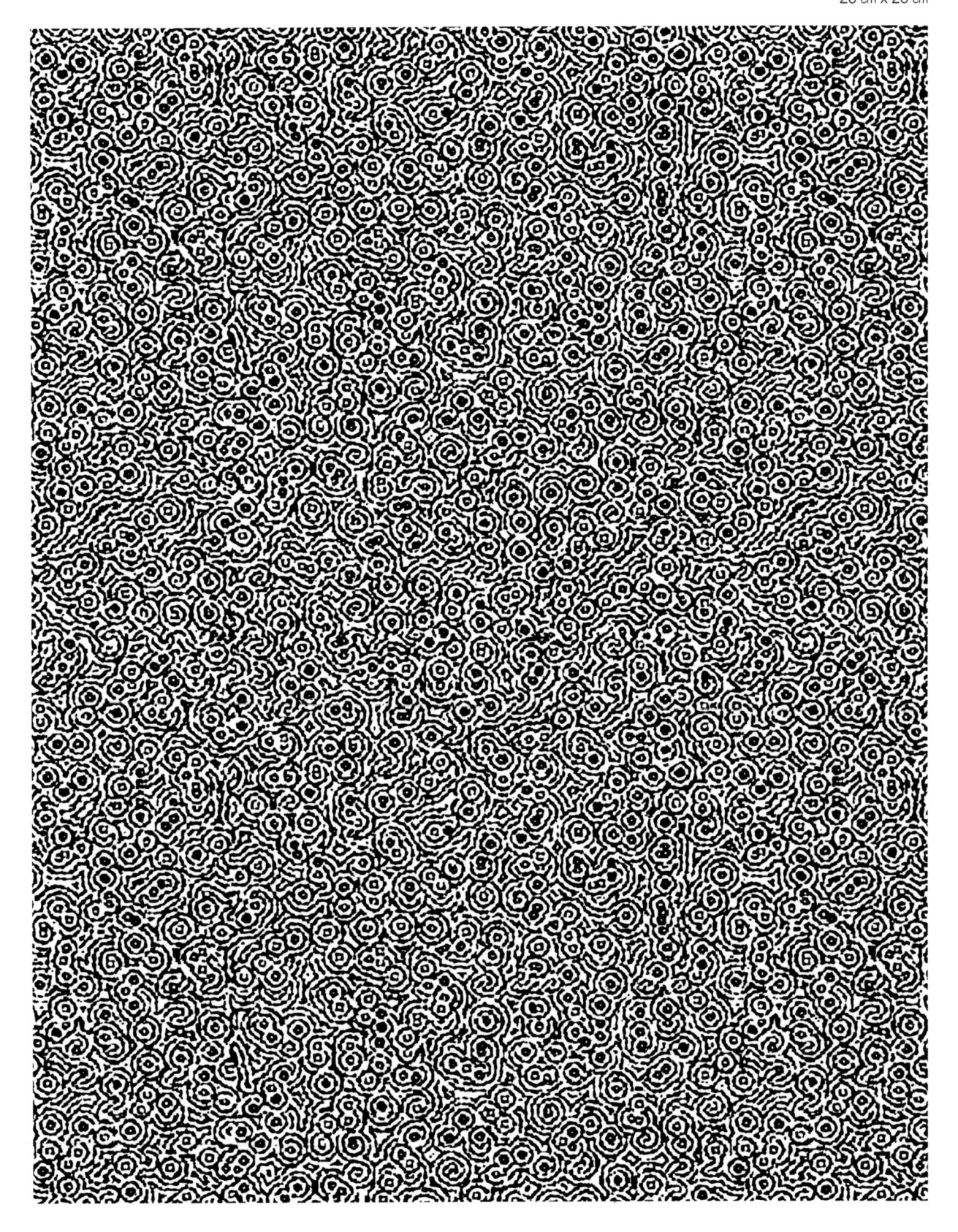

GT0138

pattern size
20 cm x 20 cm

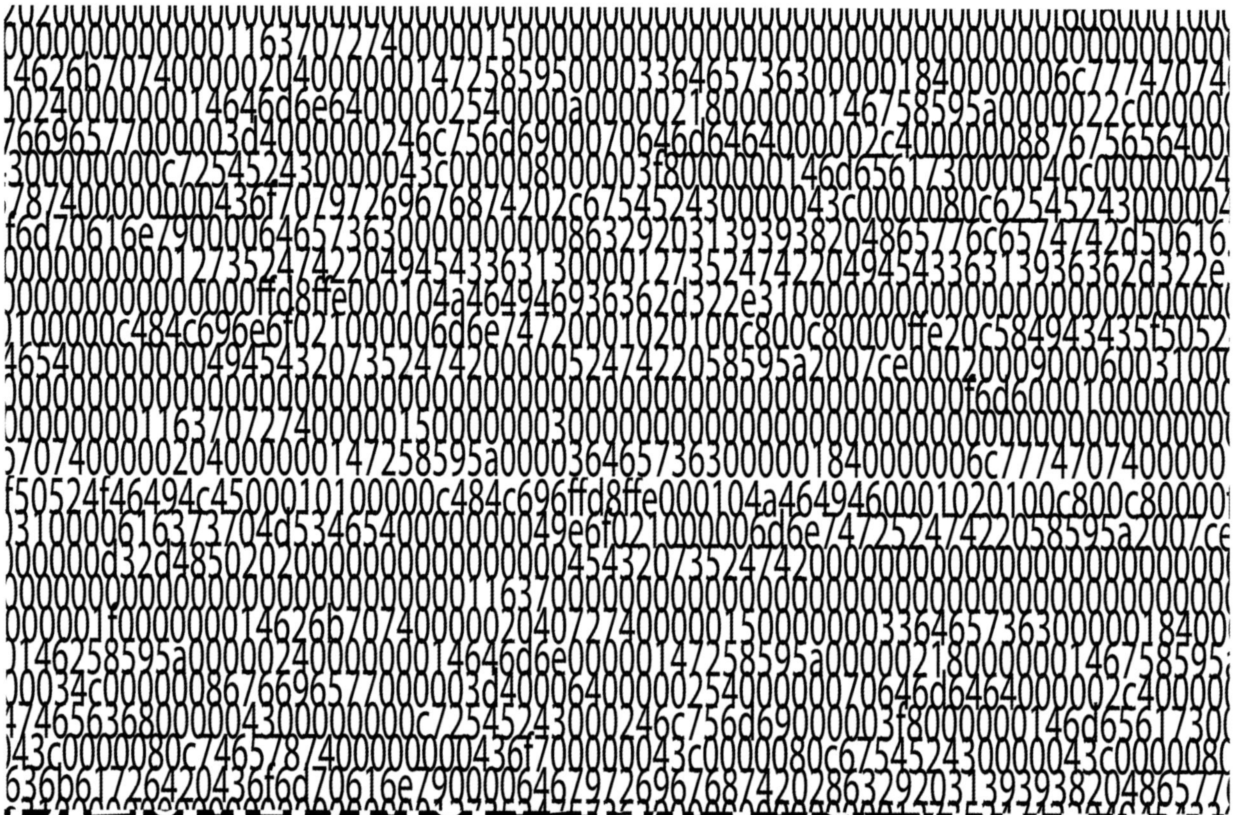

GT0139

pattern size
20 cm x 18 cm

GT0140
pattern size
20 cm x 18 cm

GT0141
pattern size
20 cm x 18 cm

117

GT0143
pattern size
35,4 cm x 35,4 cm

GT0142
pattern size
20 cm x 18 cm

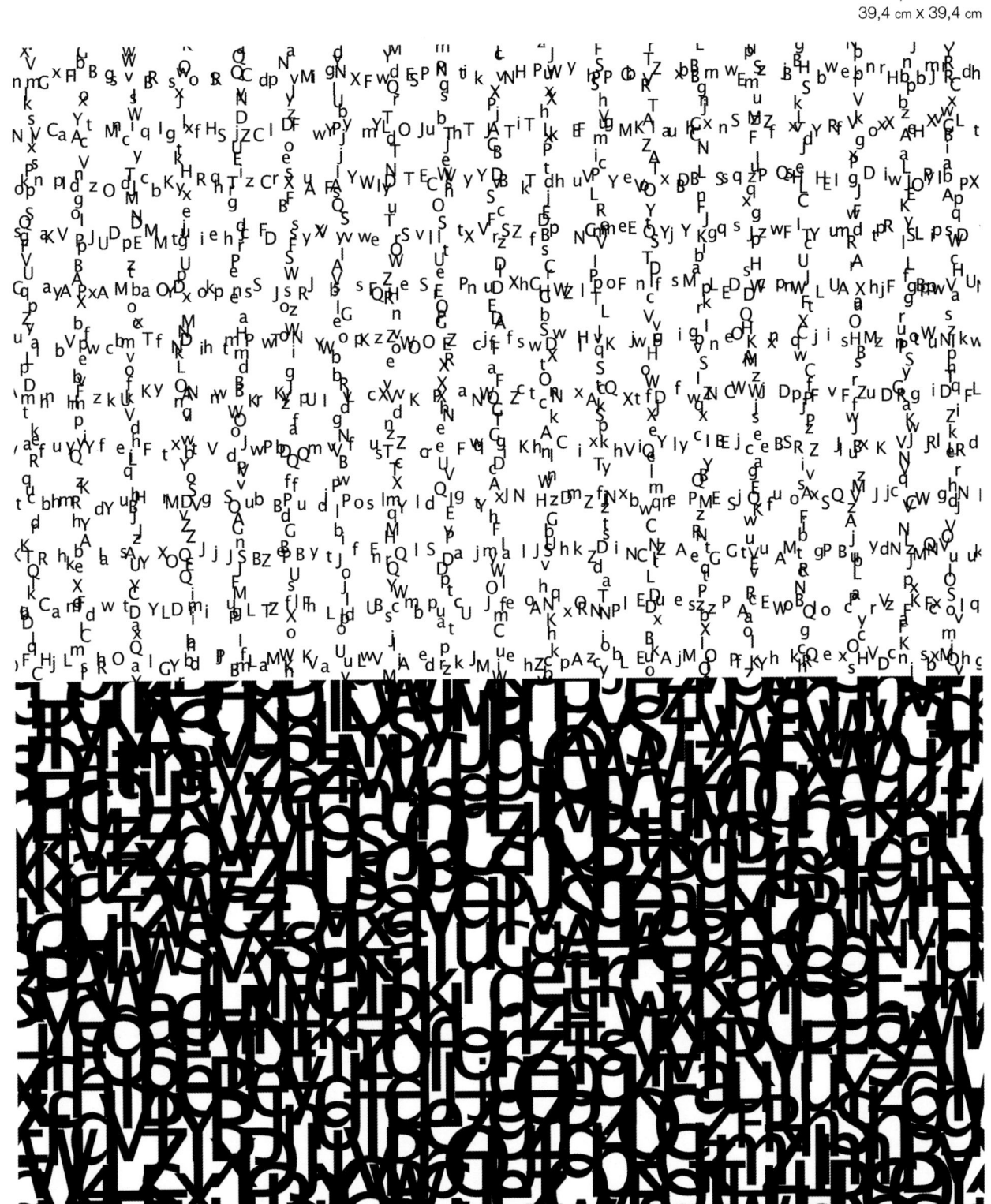

GT0144
pattern size
39,4 cm x 39,4 cm

GT0145
pattern size
34 cm x 34 cm

GT0146

pattern size
20 cm x 18 cm

GT0147

pattern size
20 cm x 18 cm

**GT0148**
pattern size
42 cm x 42 cm

**GT0149**
pattern size
20 cm x 18 cm

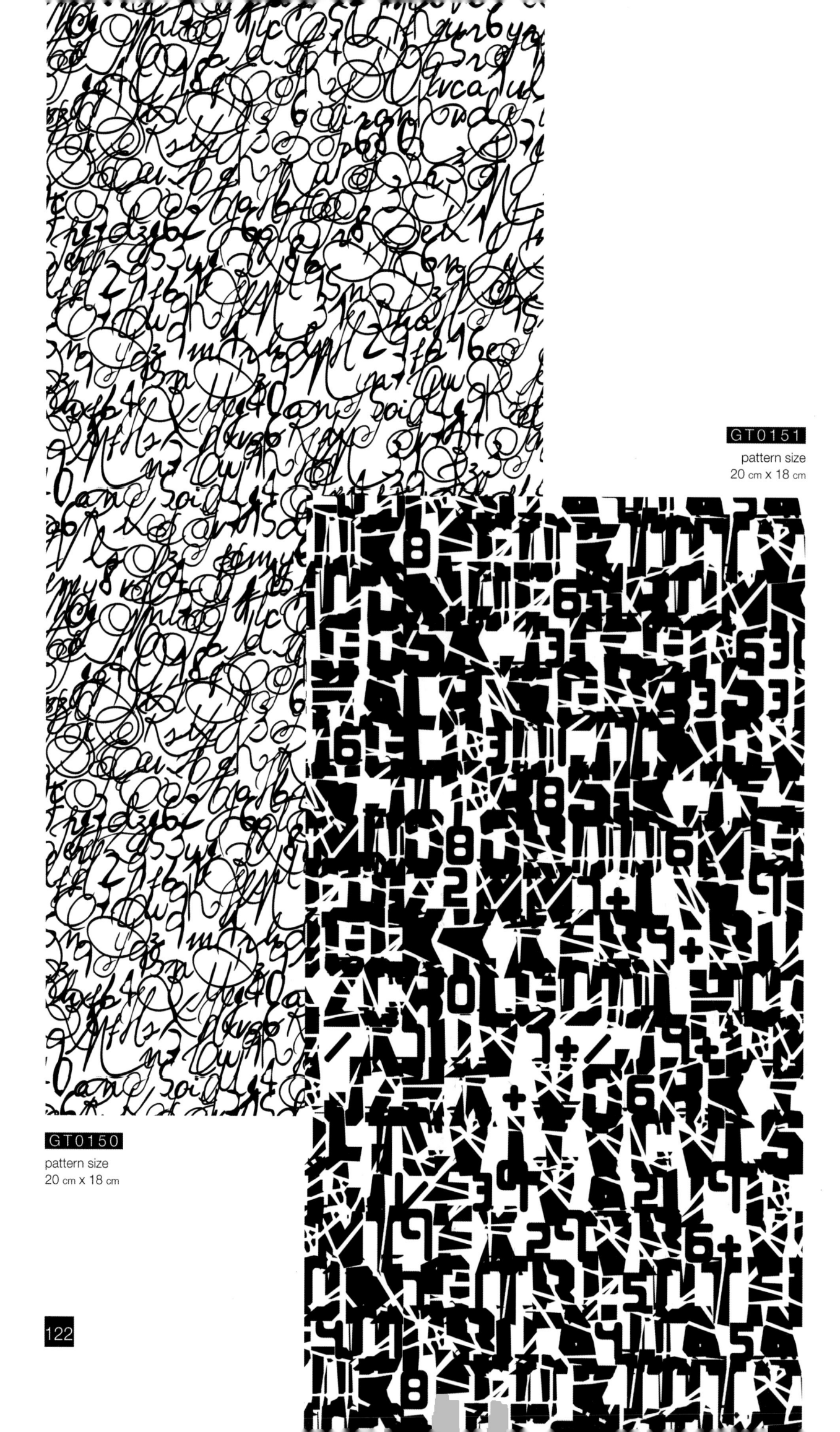

GT0151
pattern size
20 cm x 18 cm

GT0150
pattern size
20 cm x 18 cm

GT0152

pattern size
20 cm x 18 cm

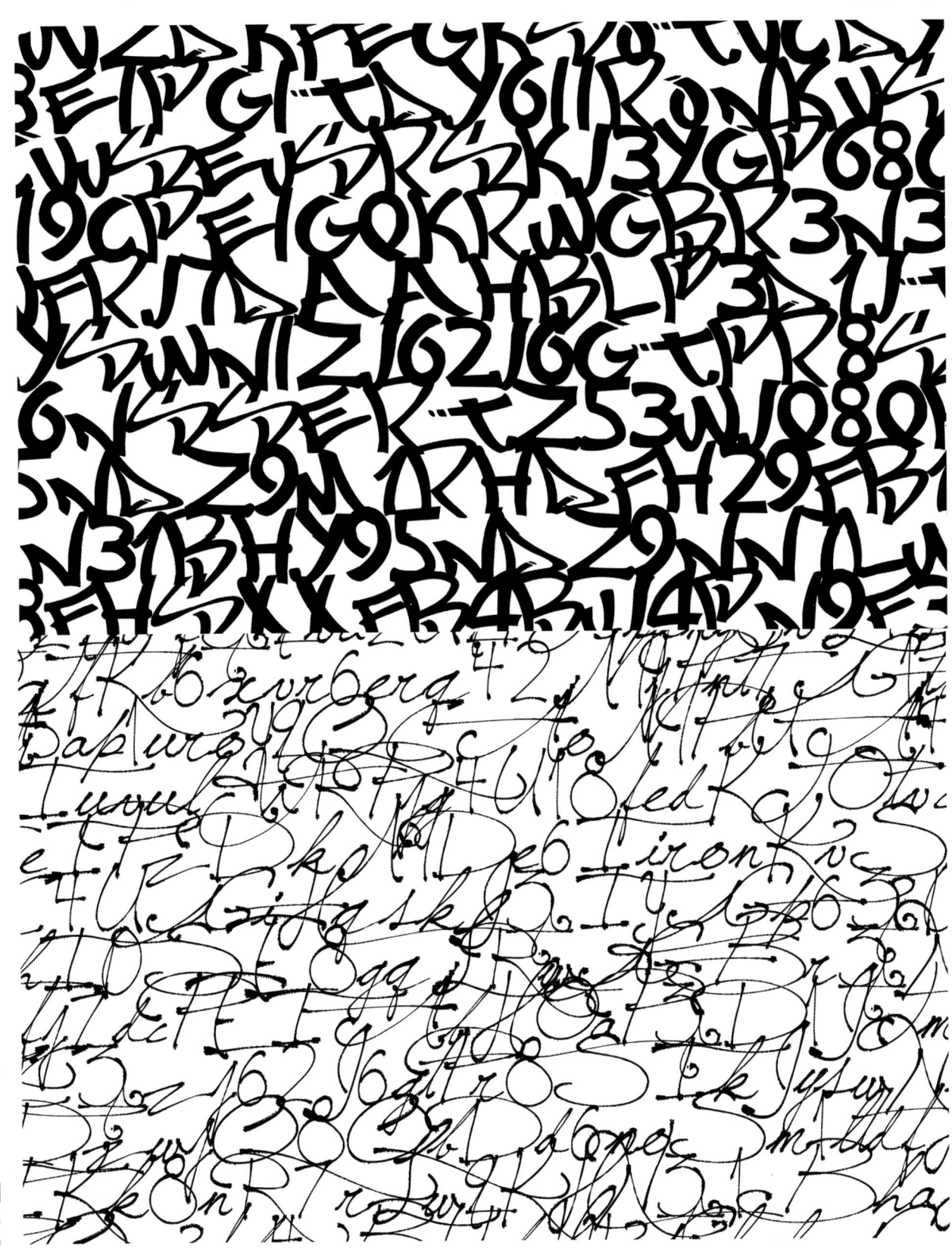

GT0153

pattern size
20 cm x 18 cm

123

GT0154
pattern size
20 cm x 18 cm

GT0155
pattern size
20 cm x 18 cm

GT0156

pattern size
20 cm x 18 cm

GT0157

pattern size
20 cm x 18 cm

125

GT0159
pattern size
20 cm x 18 cm

GT0158
pattern size
25,8 cm x 38,3 cm

GT0160

pattern size
20 cm x 30 cm

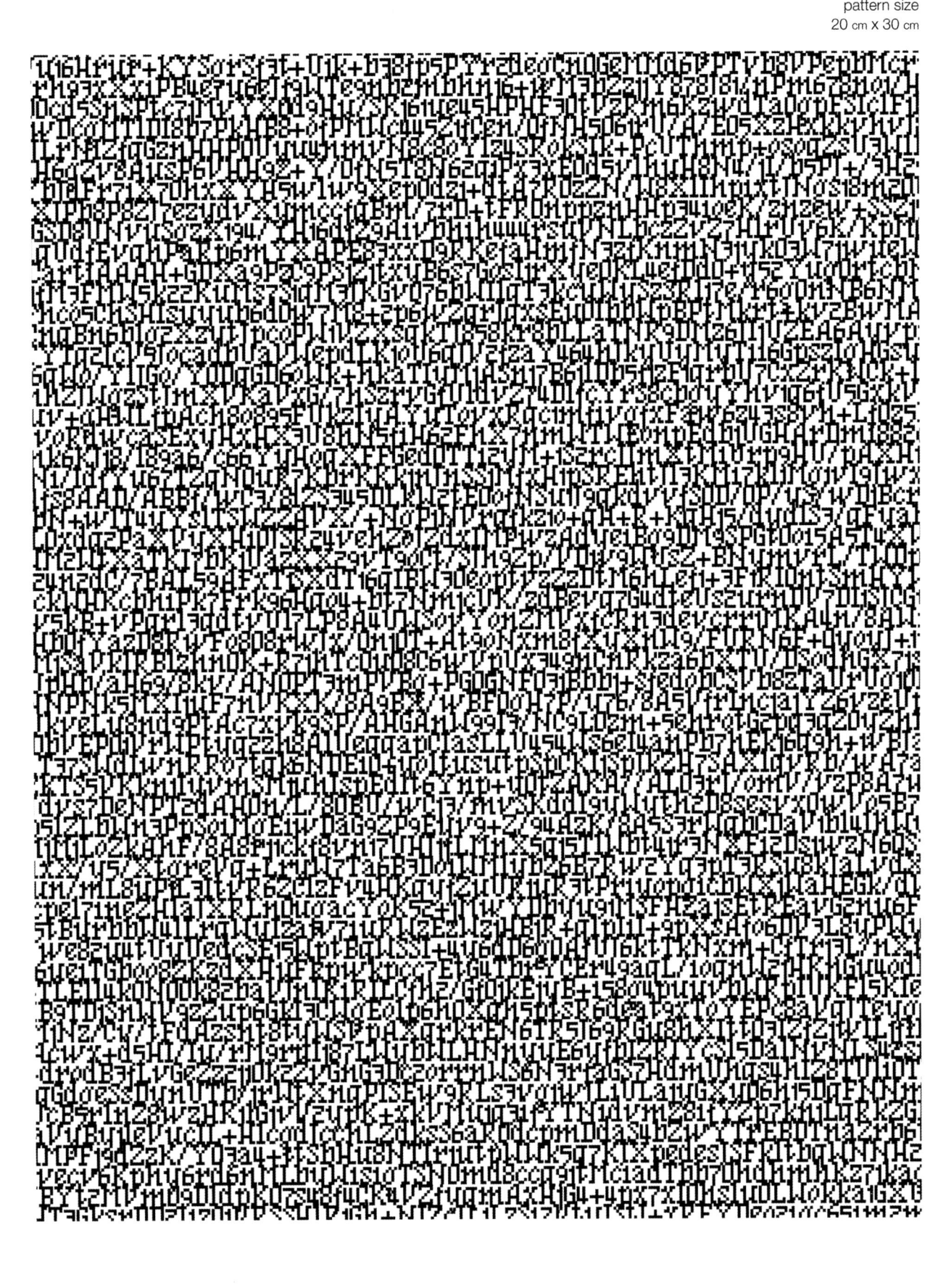

# Arkivia Books
## collection

WHY ARKIVIA BOOKS?

For those who work as stylists or designers of product lines in various merceological sectors, one of the most important jobs is to determine the look that the line should have to attract clients and distinguish itself from others.

Research is fundamental, before any design can be made, research using books, magazines, samples of objects found all over the world. This results in a large quantity of ideas on which the marketing department works before starting to develop one of them.
A long and expensive process to reach the development of the designs, keeping in mind the production methods.

I have inserted into my books this kind of know-how:

1 - Research into a tendency theme
2 - Development of creative ideas that illustrate it
3 - Professional artworks for immediate production with that look.

WHO FINDS ARKIVIA BOOKS USEFUL?

1 - Those who create products every day and need to document a single theme suitable to the product.
2 - Companies that with a small amount of money, very low compared with the high costs of creative studios, can access material ready to be used and developed by their internal staff.

In the recent past, Tendency Books have been produced for a restricted club of professional people who could afford the high cost of this sort of book
(around 1000/1500 euros).
I have decided to create books with the same spirit but within the reach of any professional in image.
As expensive as a good quality book but no more than is accepted in bookshops.

SOME TECHNICAL INFORMATION

All files in the CD or in DVD are in hi-res format: PHOTOSHOP PDF format for bitmap files or ILLUSTRATOR format for vector files, accessible by all programmes and compatible with WINDOWS and MAC.

All vectorial files are modifiable because they are the original graphics and the material is produced in a professional way and ready to use.

The designs are free to be used by those who buy the books in accordance with copyright terms present in each book.

Vincenzo Sguera

**TECNO POP TEXTURES vol.1**
ISBN 9788888766010

HARDBACK • 144 pages • size 24cm x 30.7cm
Contents:
200 Modular Patterns with 2 free CD included
Vector files in flat colors and CMYK

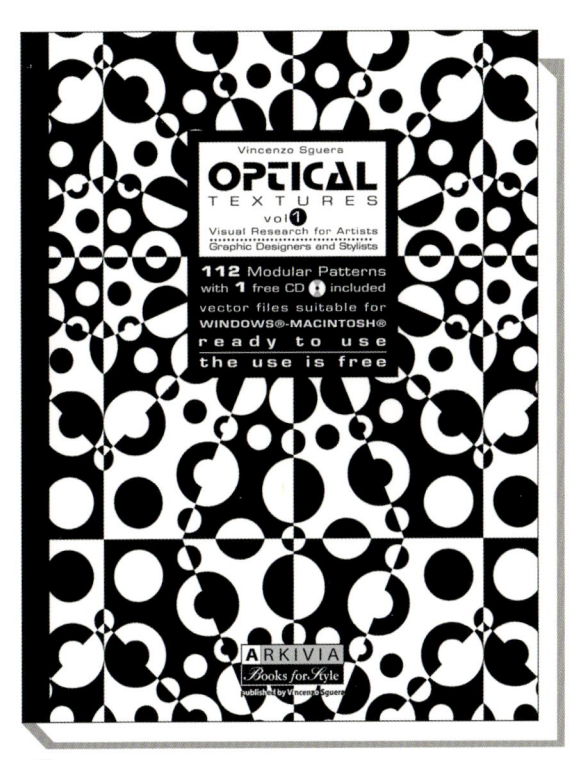

**OPTICAL TEXTURES vol.1**
ISBN 9788888766027

PAPERBACK • 128 pages • size 24cm x 30.7cm
Contents:
112 Modular Patterns with 1 free CD included
Vector files in flat colors and CMYK

**STYLING BOOK vol.1**
ISBN 9788888766034

HARDBACK • 144 pages • size 24cm x 30.7cm
Contents:
More than 600 designs with 2 free CDs included
Vector files in flat colors and CMYK

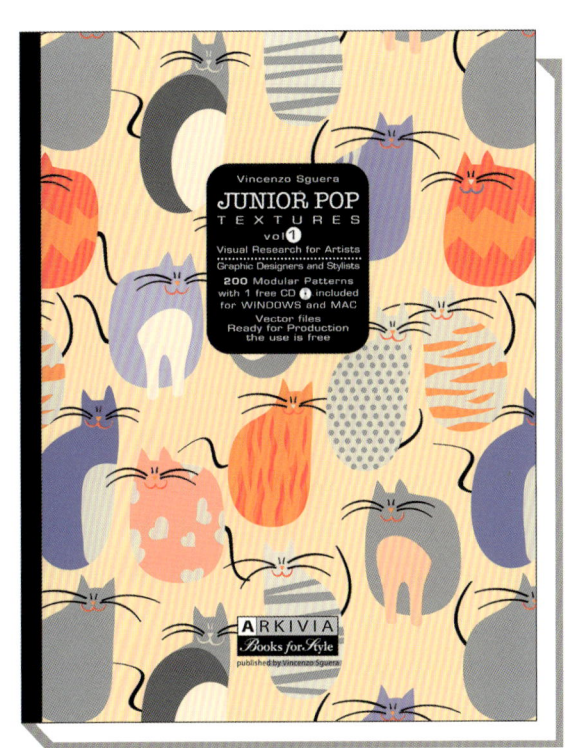

**JUNIOR POP TEXTURES vol.1**
ISBN 9788888766041

HARDBACK • 144 pages • size 24cm x 30.7cm
Contents:
200 Modular Patterns with 1 free CD included
Vector files in flat colors and CMYK

### STYLING BOOK vol.2
ISBN 9788888766058

HARDBACK • 160 pages • size 24cm x 30.7cm
Contents:
More than 500 designs with 1 free DVD included
Vector files in flat colors and CMYK

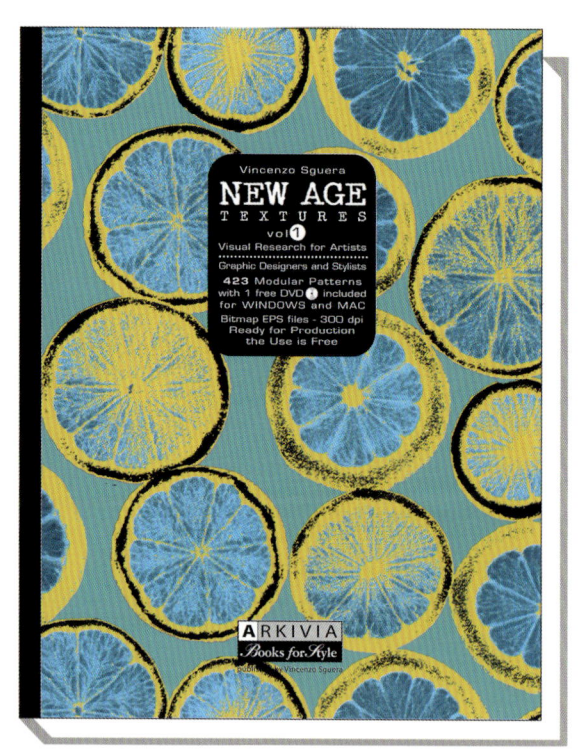

### NEW AGE TEXTURES vol.1
ISBN 9788888766065

PAPERBACK • 144 pages • size 24cm x 30.7cm
Contents:
423 Modular Patterns with 1 free DVD included
EPS Bitmap files - CMYK - 300 dpi resolution

### GOTHIC POP TEXTURES vol.1
ISBN 9788888766072

HARDBACK • 144 pages • size 24cm x 30.7cm
Contents:
130 Modular Patterns with 1 free DVD included
Vector files in flat colors and CMYK

### GOTHIC POP TEXTURES vol.2
ISBN 9788888766089

HARDBACK • 144 pages • size 24cm x 30.7cm
Contents:
130 Modular Patterns with 1 free DVD included
Vector files in flat colors and CMYK

**CHARACTER STYLING vol.1 - THE CAT**
ISBN   9788888766096

HARDBACK • 72 pages • size 24cm x 30.7cm
Contents:
216 Designs (6 Characters) with 1 free CD included
Vector files in flat colors and CMYK

**GOTHIC POP GRAPHICS vol.1**
ISBN   9788888766102

HARDBACK • 144 pages • size 24cm x 30.7cm
Contents:
132 Graphics with 1 free DVD included
Vector files in flat colors and CMYK

**NATURAL POP TEXTURES vol.1**
ISBN   9788888766119

HARDBACK • 144 pages • size 24cm x 30.7cm
Contents:
130 Textures with 1 free DVD included
Vector files in flat colors and CMYK

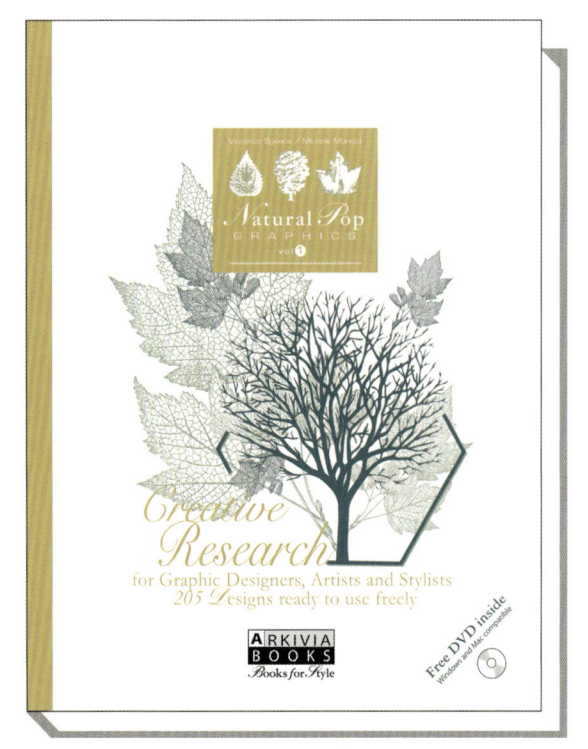

**NATURAL POP GRAPHICS vol.1**
ISBN   9788888766126

HARDBACK • 144 pages • size 24cm x 30.7cm
Contents:
205 Graphics with 1 free DVD included
Vector files in flat colors and CMYK

**CHARACTER STYLING vol.2-THE BEAR**
ISBN   9788888766133

HARDBACK • 72 pages • size 24cm x 30.7cm
Contents:
222 Designs (8 Characters) with 1 free CD included
Vector files in flat colors and CMYK

**BLACK & WHITE MATRIX 1**
ISBN   9788888766140

HARDBACK • 144 pages • size 24cm x 30.7cm
Contents:
325 Textures with 1 free DVD included
Vector files in flat colors and CMYK

**MATRIX GRAPHIX 1**
ISBN   9788888766157

HARDBACK • 144 pages • size 24cm x 30.7cm
Contents:
250 Graphics with 1 free DVD included
Vector files in flat colors and CMYK

**BLACK & WHITE MATRIX 2**
ISBN   9788888766164

HARDBACK • 144 pages • size 24cm x 30.7cm
Contents:
275 Textures with 1 free DVD included
Vector files in flat colors and CMYK

**ULTRA POP TEXTURES vol. 1**
ISBN 9788888766188

HARDBACK • 144 pages • size 24cm x 30.7cm
Contents:
130 Textures with 1 free CD included
Vector files in flat colors and CMYK

The essence of the eighties, strong and varied, is the mix. Even in a provocative way in order to find new roads, roads that have signposted the present time, such as the Postmodern Look in contraposition to the elegant Minimalism of HI-TECH or Optical matched with Floreal, geometries and chaotic puzzles. Colours and Contrasts. This is ULTRAPOP.

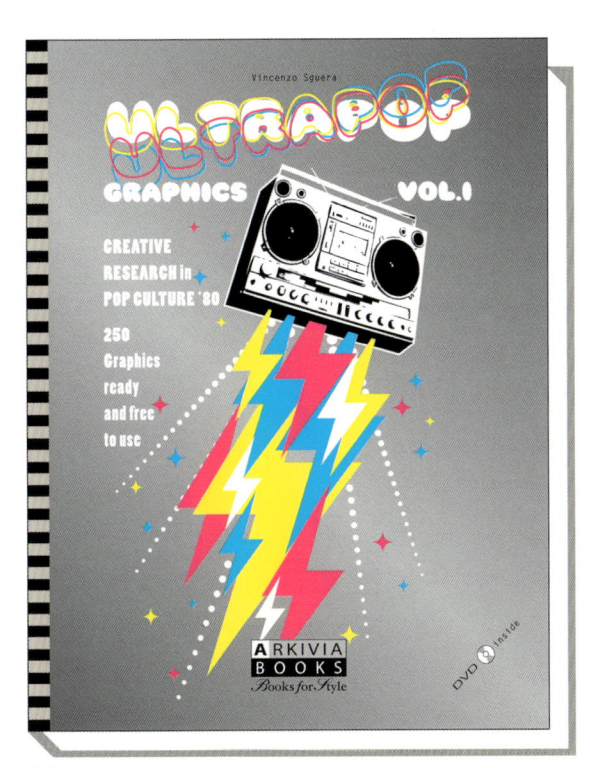

**ULTRA POP GRAPHICS vo. 1**
ISBN 9788888766195

HARDBACK • 144 pages • size 24cm x 30.7cm
Contents:
250 Graphics with 1 free DVD included
Vector files in flat colors and CMYK

The graphics of the '80s had the strength to transform a product combining circle and triangle, soft curves and broken lines.
Decisive colours with a lot of black in attendance, many nets, pois, lines and optical effects, mixing photos and designs, ancient and modern.
New fonts were beginning to be used, the need was not yet obvious, but unconscious.
These were the Eighties, this is ULTRAPOP.

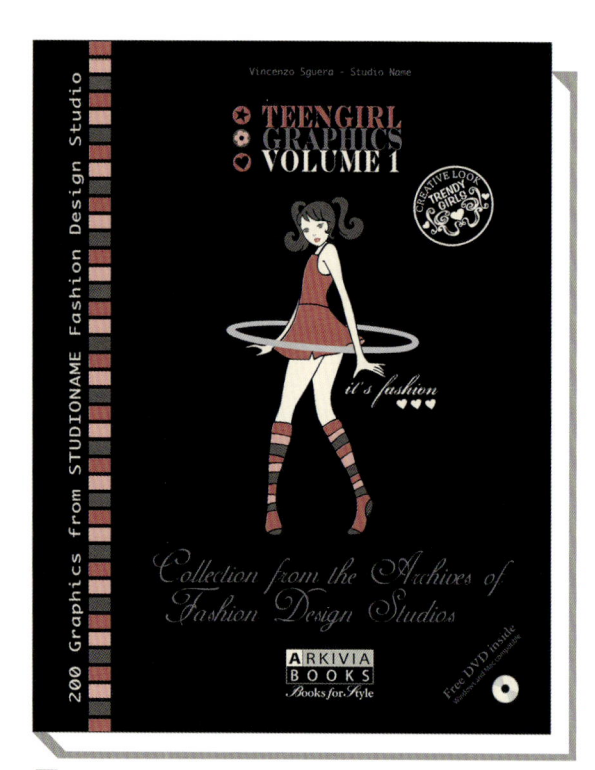

**TEEN GIRL GRAPHICS volume 1**
ISBN 9788888766171

HARDBACK • 96 pages • size 24cm x 30.7cm
Contents:
200 Graphics with 1 free CD included
Vector files in flat colors and CMYK

This book is the first of a series dedicated to Stylistic Studios which have produced so much creativity, applied to the market and used by countless firms. This project stems from a studio with many years of experience which has agreed to make public its fantastic work.
For a young and female target in a series of prints made in these last few years for important clothing firms.

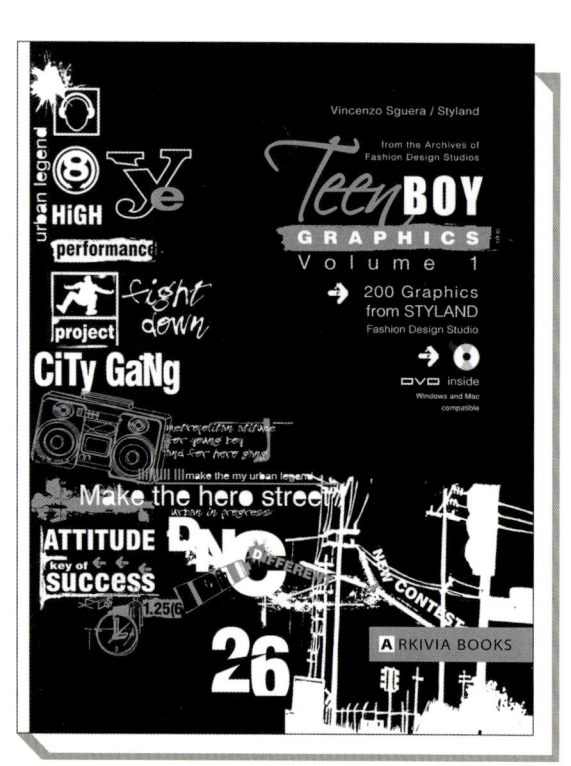

**TEEN BOY GRAPHICS volume 1**
ISBN 9788888766225

HARDBACK • 144 pages • size 24cm x 30.7cm
Contents:
200 Graphics with 1 free DVD included
Vector files in flat colors and CMYK

This book is the second of a series dedicated to Stylistic Studios which have produced so much creativity, applied to the market and used by countless firms.
This title deals with the young and male target in a series of prints made in these last few years.
ARKIVIA BOOKS is happy to share with other creative people this imaginative source of highly professional ideas.

## JUNIOR POP GRAPHICS VOL.1

ISBN 9788888766201
HARDBACK • 96 pages
size 24cm x 30.7cm
Already Available

213 GRAPHICS saved in 5 ways
1065 files in all
1 Free DVD included
for WINDOWS and MAC
Vector and Bitmap Files

Graphics for children that portray our world in a happy way, without dramatization and full of joy and delight.

On every page a Unique Brand, a strong idea to depart from and as we know, for a creative person, the world of children is a journey without end.

## Ethno Pop Textures vol.1

**ISBN 9788888766218**
HARDBACK • 112 pages
size 24cm x 30.7cm
Already Available

100 TEXTURES saved in 5 ways
500 files in all
1 Free DVD included
for WINDOWS and MAC
Vector and Bitmap Files
Ready for Production
The use is Free

## Ethno Pop Textures vol.2

**ISBN 9788888766263**
HARDBACK • 112 pages
size 24cm x 30.7cm
Publication Date: Summer 2014

100 TEXTURES saved in 5 ways
500 files in all
1 Free DVD included
for WINDOWS and MAC
Vector and Bitmap Files
Ready for Production
The use is Free

## Ultra Pop Textures vol.2

**ISBN 9788888766232**

HARDBACK • 144 pages
size 24cm x 30.7cm
Already Available

120 TEXTURES saved in
5 ways - 600 files in all.
1 Free DVD included
for WINDOWS and MAC
Vector and Bitmap Files
Ready and Free to Use.
They can be used
with many graphic softwares
such as ILLUSTRATOR or
PHOTOSHOP.

These designs describe a
path which covers 3 decades
from the 60 s to the 80 s.

They highlight a very special
decorative taste, at the same
time refined and naif, floral
and geometric in unison.
Designs that communicate
the rhythm of an epoch full
of colours and elegance.

There is a need for amusing
creativity, a need for
ULTRA POP TEXTURES.

## Natural Pop Textures vol.2

**ISBN** 9788888766270

HARDBACK • 144 pages
size 24cm x 30.7cm
Already Available

122 TEXTURES saved in
5 ways - 610 files in all.
1 Free DVD included
for WINDOWS and MAC
Vector and Bitmap Files
Ready and Free to Use.
They can be used with
many graphic softwares
such as ILLUSTRATOR
or PHOTOSHOP.

This second book develops
more soft and elegant designs
inspired by modern
North-European Design
also called Scandinavian Style.

Graphic synthesis, clean and
essential, is preferred to
realistic representation,
which is less suitable for home
decoration, interior design and
fashion clothing textiles.
Many new ideas in delicate
and harmonious colours in
tune with the present market.

## Animal Style Textures vol.1

**ISBN** 9788888766294

HARDBACK • 160 pages
size 24cm x 30.7cm
Already Available

154 TEXTURES saved in
5 ways - 770 files in all.
1 Free DVD included
for WINDOWS and MAC
Vector and Bitmap Files
Ready and Free to Use.

There is a tendency that has slowly but surely imposed itself: the style inspired by animal skins. Strong, essential and recognizable it has managed to renew itself, passing from a simple proposal of natural skins to mixing these in a fresh and new way.

These designs can be used with many graphic softwares such as ILLUSTRATOR or PHOTOSHOP.

Already Available

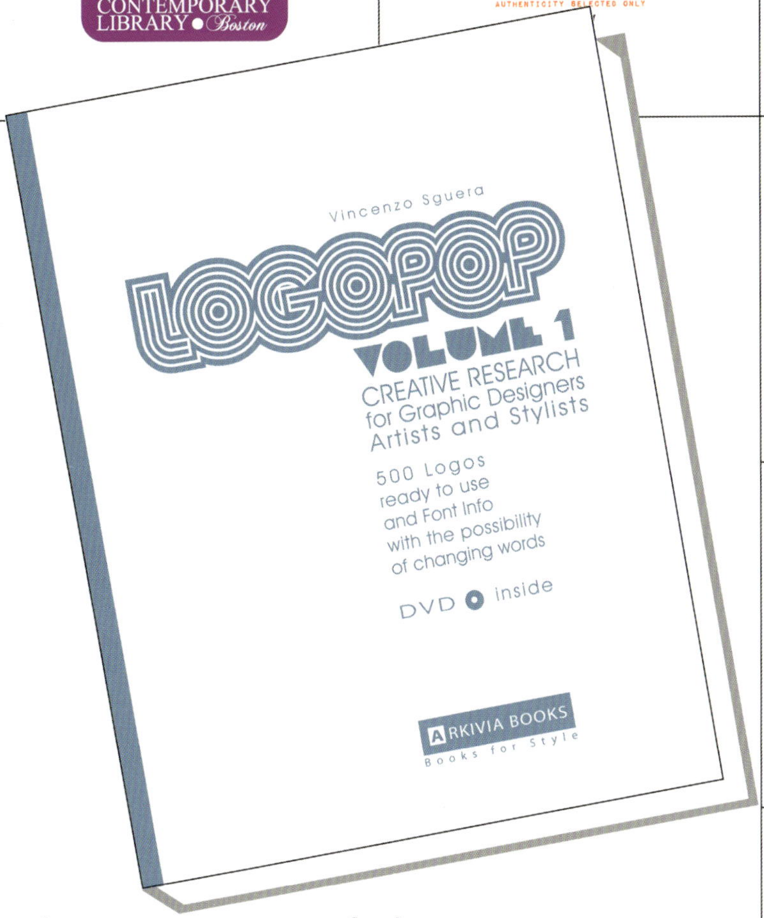

## Logopop vol.1 ISBN 9788888766256
HARDBACK • 160 pages • 24cm x 30.7cm

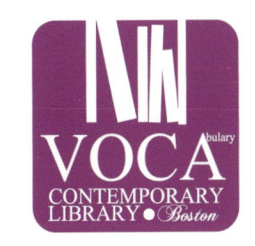

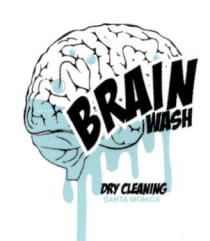

**500 Logos ready to use and font info with the possibility of changing words.**

In the panorama of books which offer hundreds if not thousands of Logos and Brands, there has always been a lack of one with new and original designs, with the possibility of use.
This would have satisfied anyone, but I realized that if the word used for a brand could not be utilized either because of creative choice or for copyright reasons, then the inserted designs would only be partially useful.
To avoid this, I decided that the projects should offer the possibility of changing the text, so that the brand could be personalized, using a chosen word.
I have therefore used only freeware fonts, downloaded free from the Internet to allow you to change the words, if you wish, and I have cited the link where you can download the font used.
Also enclosed in the DVD there is a file in Excel where you can link directly each font to download it. Make your own Logo!

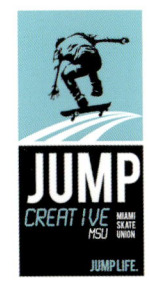

## Kinetic Art Textures vol.1

**ISBN** 9788888766287

**HARDBACK** • 144 pages
size 24cm x 30.7cm
Already Available

120 TEXTURES saved in
5 ways - 600 files in all.
1 Free DVD included
for WINDOWS and MAC
Vector and Bitmap Files
Ready and Free to Use.
They can be used
with many graphic softwares
such as ILLUSTRATOR or
PHOTOSHOP.

Beyond the image and the meaning in every work, there are rhythm and structure to catch the aesthetics abstracted from the meaning. The geometries have their own values apart from what they represent but when they describe Life, they do so in a continuous and rhythmic way. This need for abstract art through movement is known as "KINETIC ART". Designs with merely the beauty of line and structure.

## Flower Fashion Textures vol.1

**ISBN 9788888766300**

HARDBACK • 144 pages
size 24cm x 30.7cm
Already Available

300 TEXTURES saved in
5 ways - 1500 files in all.
1 Free DVD included
for WINDOWS and MAC
Vector and Bitmap Files
Ready and Free to Use.
They can be used with
many graphic softwares
such as ILLUSTRATOR or
PHOTOSHOP.

The world of Fashion has
always drawn inspiration from
nature, colors and decorations.
Small and large flowers with
stripes and squares or
provençal and oriental designs.
Roses and violets, poppies and
daisies in a continuous flow of
textures, designed from scratch
to make vectorial and more
synthetic designs following the
trend of present graphics.

A unique work, long but exciting
for variety and ideas, ready to
be used in a host of products
for all targets.

# BLACK AND WHITE MATRIX 3

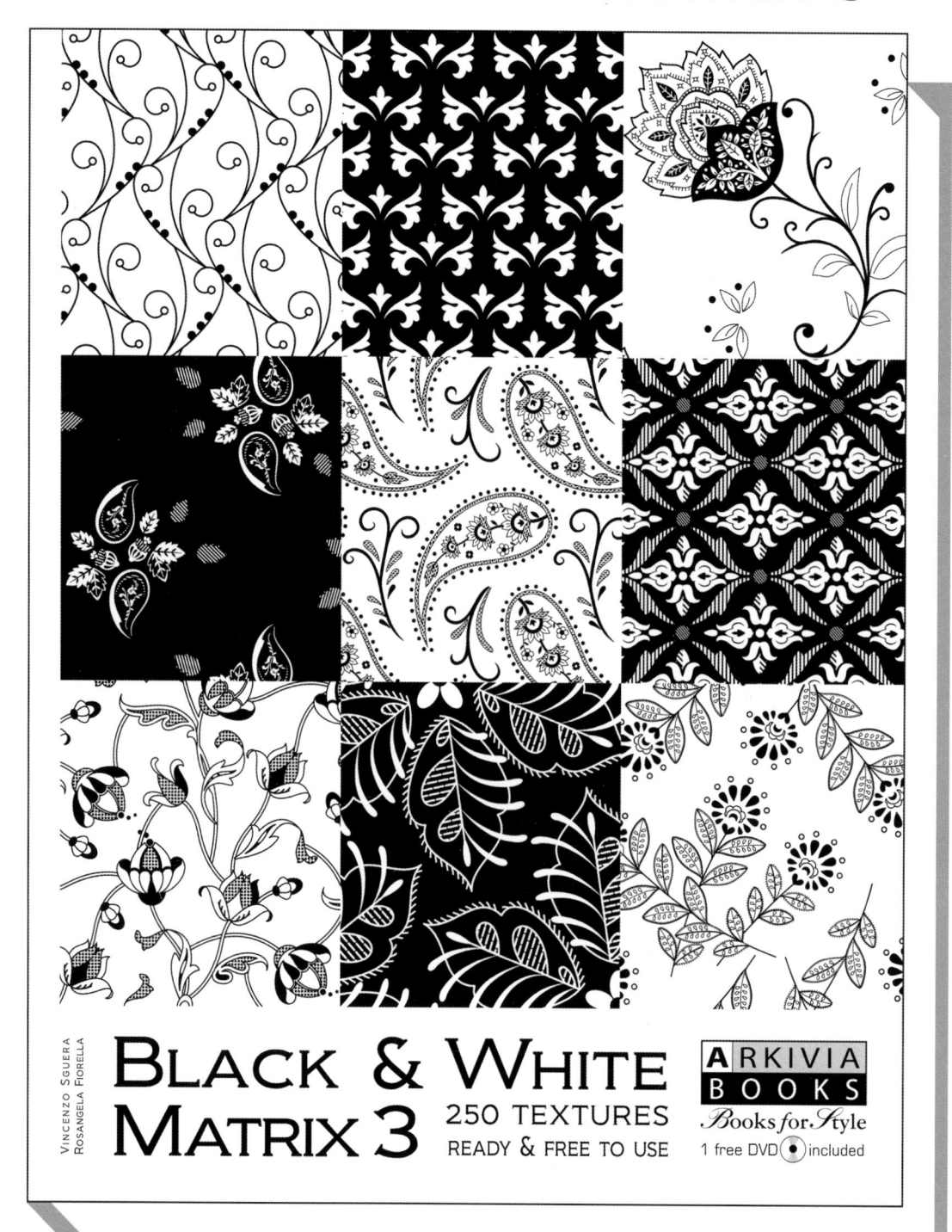

**Black & White Matrix 3**
250 TEXTURES
READY & FREE TO USE

Vincenzo Sguera
Rosangela Fiorella

ARKIVIA BOOKS
Books for Style
1 free DVD included

**ISBN 9788888766317**
HARDBACK • 144 pages
size 24cm x 30.7cm
Publication Date: Winter 2014

250 TEXTURES saved in 5 ways
1250 files in all
1 Free DVD included
for WINDOWS and MAC
Vector and Bitmap Files
Ready for Production
The use is Free

When decorative cultures from far away places meet.
Europe and Asia with their traditions may coexist and adopt a mature look. Various decorative layers and backgrounds, rich in detail, lead beyond the level of taste bringing us to appreciate compositions never attempted before, a more graphic and essential pot pourri.
They can be used with many graphic softwares, such as ILLUSTRATOR or PHOTOSHOP.